5 ROADS, DITTON HILL, SURREY.

LONG DITTON
REMEMBERED

*L*ONG *Ditton is a remarkable village, for in the shadows of its graceful horse chestnut trees, towering pines and age-old oaks is a little community which has managed to retain much of what has made it pleasant for so many years. Friendly shopkeepers, happy schools and cheery neighbours have all played their part in making Long Ditton special.*

Historically, the village has been on the map for at least 1,000 years and it has often been pointed out that it is 'older' than neighbouring Thames Ditton. Regrettably, some of its most remarkable buildings like the old Rectory have been bulldozed. Others like Upper Ditton House, the old School House, Chalcott, Pound Farm and Saxonbury have also been pulled down but in many cases their names have been immortalised in the titles of the cul-de-sacs which replace them.

Furthermore, some public houses have been lost forever. The Three Pigeons and the Crown and Anchor now belong to an era when labourers at the waterworks and wharfs called to quench their thirst after a long day at work. In the pages which follow, re-live those days in Long Ditton and imagine what it must have been like in the times long before videos, mobile phones and the Internet.

Filling up with fuel at Roots Motors (Long Ditton Motors Ltd) 122 Portsmouth Road, Long Ditton, c1965.

Labour Prime Minister Harold Wilson used to visit Woodstock, Woodstock Lane, in the late 1960s when the residential college was run by the National Union of General and Municipal Workers.

Lollipop lady Mrs Margaret Lyle, from Rushett Close, started seeing children safely across the Ditton Hill Road in 1986 and continued this position during the 1990s.

Acknowledgements

Peter Fussell and the wardens of St Mary's Church, Long Ditton; David Tippett-Wilson; Fred and Pat Rainbow; Rev Eric Smith; Kingston Local History Centre's Gill Lamb and Tim Everson; The Dittons Library staff; National Tramway Museum staff, Crich, Derbyshire; Surrey Postal History Society's W H Legg; Miss Hooper, of Littlecot; Percy Perrin; David Saunders; Alison Saunders; Mrs Sue Woods and the staff of St Mary's Junior School, Long Ditton; I McCallum, of Claygate; Alan Rackley; June Sampson and the Surrey Comet staff; Mrs Brenda Carr of Ember Antiques, Thames Ditton; John Janaway and staff at the now-defunct Surrey Local Studies Library, Guildford; John Callan, of the Ferry Tavern; Brian and Eva Arnold; Rae Burgess; Maggie Hayles and staff at the Forge Pet Supplies; Bob and Elsie Clark; Reg Driver; the late T S Mercer; Patrick Bennett; Marion Bone; Paul Gower, of The Maypole; Pat Knight; Mary Solomons; Peter Butler; Arthur Lucking and Pat Thompson of Thorkhill Road; M and N Davison; Nigel Davison; Mrs Fussell; Maggie Vaughan-Lewis and staff at the County Records Office, Kingston; various members of St Mary's Church; London Omnibus Traction Society; Richard Shirley; George Peter Thomas Muggleton; Dave Swan; Philip Butler, the Seven Slovakian Sisters and Mrs Nora Adams of Ditton Hill Road for the chocolate biscuits and late-night cups of Milo after heavy research sessions.

Photograph credits

Surrey Local Studies Library, (1950s and 1960s views of shops); Fred Rainbow collection; Paul Adams; St Mary's Church archives; Peter Fussell; Dittons Library collection; Surrey Comet for tram timetable adverts; National Tramway Museum, Crich; Esher News and Mail (1979 traders); Mark Davison collection; David Tippett-Wilson collection; St Mary's C of E School, Mrs Sue Woods and staff; Alison and David Saunders; Elmbridge Museum; Kingston Local History Centre; T S Mercer collection; Roy Adams; Peter Butler; the late Hetty Hatchard; the Plough and Harrow staff; W H Legg and the Surrey Postal History Society; Ian McCallum; Pat Knight; Essex Arms staff; John Callan; Bob and Elsie Clark; Brian and Eva Arnold.

Bibliography

T S Mercer collection; Richard Jefferies' nature notes; Thomas Hardy, A Biography, by Michael Millgate (Oxford University Press 1982); Rev Eric Smith's history of St Mary's parish to mark centenary of the latest church 1980; Fish Off The Slab, by Peter Fussell; magazines of St Mary's church and articles by Peter Fussell; the Surrey Comet; Kingston Borough News; Esher News and Mail; Epsom Herald; Charles 'Jack' Mason's recollections in "Reminiscences of Long Ditton"; St Mary's Church archival documents and letters; T S Mercer's local history publications; An Old Fashioned Miss, by Nellie Trouncer (1939); Miss Sybil Trouncer's diaries; The Story of Hook In Kingston by Marion Bone (1989) and Eastern Pilgrims by Margaret and Agnes Smith (1870).

Editorial assistance by Nigel Davison and Donald MacPhail

Published by Mark Davison, North Bank, Smoke Lane, Reigate, Surrey, RH2 7HJ

Printed by Litho Techniques (Kenley), Godstone Road, Whyteleafe, Surrey

ISBN 0 9534240 0 6

© Copyright October 1998

Special thanks

I AM indebted to Peter Fussell, Roy and Paul Adams and David Tippett-Wilson for their valuable assistance. Peter Fussell's published articles and booklets on the ancient parish history have provided a valuable source of information. Roy's painstaking research into the past names of all houses in Long Ditton has been an immeasurable aid. His brother, Paul's postcard collection and anecdotes have added much interest while David Tippett-Wilson's knack for locating rare photos has once again come up trumps.

This book is dedicated to Peter Fussell, whose 70th birthday was celebrated on 22nd July 1998. Peter's infectious enthusiasm for Long Ditton's history has been a great inspiration to me. I would also like to dedicate this work to the memory of Miss Sybil Tranter, the late headmistress of Long Ditton (St Mary's) School whose joie de vivre has shone through the recollections of many of her former pupils.

Peter Fussell.   *Roy Adams.*   *Paul Adams.*   *David Tippett-Wilson.*

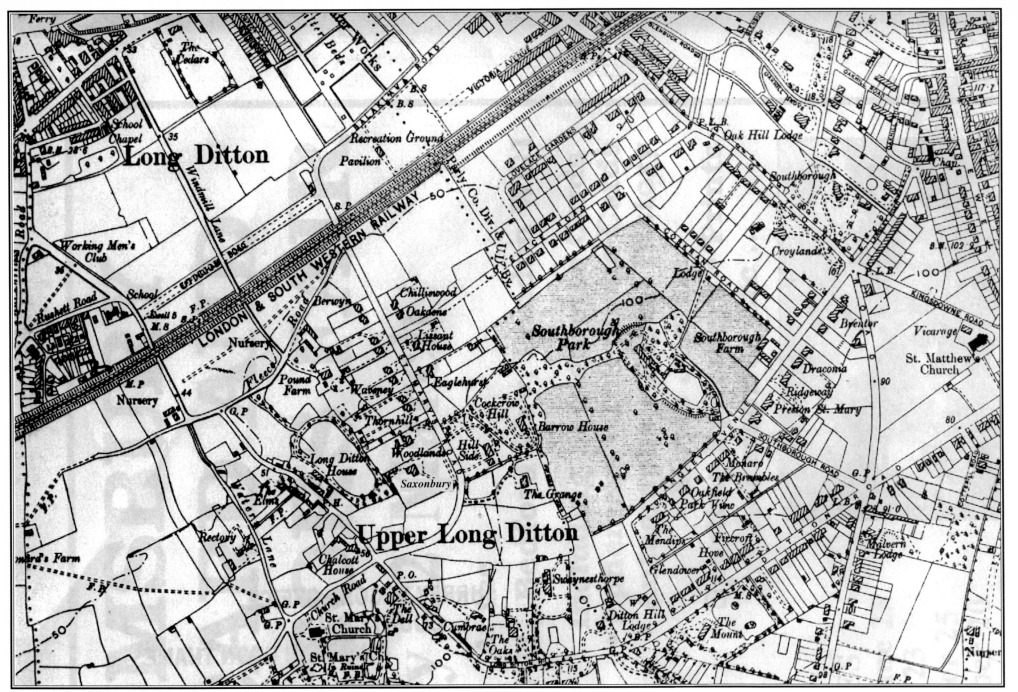

The Ordnance Survey map of the Ditton Hill area in 1895 showing some of the large houses which have long since disappeared.

Elms, kingfishers and yellowhammers

Woodstock Lane beauty

EVEN in modern times, Woodstock Lane has retained much of its rustic charm and many of its open fields.

This ancient lane between Long Ditton and Claygate was described affectionately by country writer Richard Jefferies in the 1870s.

Originally from Wiltshire, he moved to Ewell Road, Tolworth, near the junction of Ditton Road, in 1877 with his wife and first child.

From here, he used to go on rambles around Long Ditton and write of the beautiful sights he saw as he strolled down the local lanes.

One of his jottings is believed to refer to the dip in muddy Love Lane just before it joins Woodstock Lane.

He wrote of the profusion of bird life in this spot which had ponds on either side of the track *(one in the open meadows and the other in the Manor House grounds)*.

Jefferies wrote: "Standing there a minute to see if there was a martin among the birds with which the pond in the grounds is thickly covered, something came shooting straight towards me and, swerving only a yard or two to pass me, a kingfisher went by. His blue wings, his ruddy front, the white streak beside his neck, and long bill were all visible for a moment; then he was away straight over the meadow, the directness of his course enabling it to be followed for some time till he cleared the distant hedge, probably going to visit his nest . . ."

And in another reference to the same spot, Jefferies wrote: "This hollow at Long Ditton is the very place of singing birds; never was such a place for singing — the valley is full of music. In the oaks, blackbirds whistle. You do not often see them; they seek the top branches which are more leafy.

"The thrushes sing louder here than anywhere . . . warblers and wrens sing out of sight among the trees . . . greenfinches in the elms never cease love-making and love-making needs much soft talking . . . yellowhammers call from the trees up towards the arable fields . . . there is a nightingale in a bush by the lane which sings so loud the hawthorn seems to shake with the vigour of his song."

A winter's trot in Woodstock Lane near Surbiton Golf Course in about 1930. For centuries, this rural lane linked Long Ditton and Claygate but increasing traffic on the Kingston bypass in the 1960s necessitated the closure of the through route except to cyclists and pedestrians who could continue their journey by using a subway. The parish of Long Ditton took in Waffrons Farm and the golf course.

Long Ditton farmhands Stan Rainbow, left, and his father, Albert, using a horse-drawn Bamford binder in the early 1900s. The Rainbow family were true "Dittonites". Stan's nephew, Fred, lived all his life in Long Ditton — most of it at 6, Rectory Lane. Although chiefly working for Broom's Farm, Summerfield Lane, Ditton Hill, Stan and Albert also mowed Scott's Farm, Sugden Road.

Long Ditton Rectory dated back to the 16th century. Costly to run, it was sold in 1936 and demolished. Rectory Close was built on the site.

The Rectory, Long Ditton, in May 1925, as seen from a path which crossed the field at the top of Rectory Lane and led to Sugden Road.

Long Ditton's Tudor rectory

ONE of Long Ditton's oldest and largest homes was the medieval Rectory. Possibly dating back to as early as 1539, when Henry VIII was king, the rambling half-timber house had passage-ways, large dark rooms with log fires, stained glass windows, a barn, granary and summer house.

It is also said to have had a ghost of a man wearing Puritan attire.

The upstairs rooms overhung the ground floor by two feet. The Rectory stood in some six acres of beautiful countryside on the site of today's Rectory Close and was home to more than 20 rectors over 400 years.

There were a number of additions to the building over the years. The interior was rearranged and refitted in the 18th century and modern wings constructed.

The original plan appears to have been of an L-shape with the main portion lying east-west.

In the main building were two main rooms with large fireplaces. In the 18th century, a staircase was put in one of the rooms and in the other was a passage on its south side from the stair hall to a door or wing which was eventually replaced by a drawing room wing at the west end.

Reverend Alfred Martell, Rector of Long Ditton from 1906 to 1921, relaxing with his dogs in the old Rectory garden on a summer's afternoon. In 1921, Rev Robert Wilson took over and was the last rector to live at the striking old building.

Haymaking at Broom's Farm, Ditton Hill

DITTON Hill Farm — or Broom's Farm as it was known — was one of the main farms in Long Ditton. The farmhouse and a number of cottages were still standing as the millennium approached, but the traditional farming methods have long-since disappeared.

The old farm, at the top of Summerfield Lane, occupied a high position in the village and from the windows could be seen views of Hook, Southborough, and the surrounding countryside. Among the workers at the farm in the early part of the 1900s were the Rainbow and Driver families. As a boy, Reg Driver recalls the rather primitive conditions in the farm cottages which had outdoor toilets which required flushing with a jug after use.

Lizzie Rainbow and her husband, Albert, are pictured above with George Goble and another farmhand.

Albert Rainbow, a thatcher by trade, often worked at Broom's Farm, Ditton Hill. His wife, Lizzie, was a midwife in Long Ditton and also tended to corpses when death occurred in families around the village. The Rainbows were originally from Hatfield, Herts.

St Mary's long history

THERE has been a church at Long Ditton for at least 1,000 years. And in that time, there have been four or more churches at the site of the present place of worship. Village historian Peter Fussell, formerly of Rectory Close, has written at length in other publications about the church's history and described in detail its times of hardship, conflict, and persecution.

A list of the rectors — or church officials in charge — goes back to 1166 when Roger Picot was at the helm.

Detailed records of the church since 1564 have been preserved and Rev Eric Smith, who arrived in 1967, also carried out much research and published a small book on his study of the chronicles.

In the 1920s, Rev Robert Wilson even indicated that Roman bricks were found in the upper churchyard.

When Richard Byfield took over in 1627, he was a Puritan and got into trouble with the Archbishop Laud for refusing to read the Book of Sports which allowed some relaxation in the observance of Sundays. In 1634 he was suspended but he was so obstinate, he continued to officiate. The church still bears the scars of the rage of the Puritans. One of the brasses salvaged from the old church can be seen to have been defaced. It bore an inscription to a former rector with the words: "Upon Whose Soul Jesu Have Mercy". These words have been obliterated — it is thought by Puritans who objected to these sentiments.

Mr Smith discovered that the parishioners of the long-distant past were sometimes a rather dull lot and consisted chiefly of "upper class gentry". He noticed that they were, however, roused greatly by plans to build a railway station in the area. They saw this as a threat to disturb or even put an end to their peaceful home life.

The railway did come. Surbiton Station opened in May 1838.

In about 1165, Archbishop St Thomas a Becket visited the church. "He rode concealed in a cloak and accompanied by one sole companion as a guide."

Above: Long Ditton Church 1776 - 1880. Below: An earlier church built in medieval times.

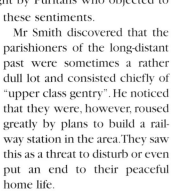

Rev Charles Hughes, rector from 1889 to 1906.

Rev Eric Smith arrived in 1967 and stayed until 1982.

Crown and Anchor

The relocated Crown and Anchor shut on 9th July 1965. It stood on the Portsmouth Road-Windmill Lane corner for almost a century. The site was bought by Comerford's for a car park. The last landlord was Reg Dixey.

ORIGINALLY the Crown and Anchor was an ancient coaching inn on Wharf Road. This road used to run behind the present City Arms in Portsmouth Road and along the river front to Thames Ditton High Street.

Wharf Road was closed in 1771 after a rich widow, the Honourable Charlotte Digby, bought the triangular piece of land bordered by the River Rythe, the Thames and Portsmouth Road, taking in Claremont Wharf. She already owned neighbouring Forde Farm and wanted to expand the estate. Irritated by Wharf Road going through her new land, she pressed the authorities to create a new road between Long Ditton and Thames Ditton — what is now St Leonard's Road.

The old Crown and Anchor in Wharf Road — named on an 1843 tithe map the Rose and Crown — was described at that time as being a public house, gardens and buildings kept by 'Widow Payne'. The widow's late husband, Charlie, had run it but he died in 1836. There was a skittle alley at the back, a garden with tables set out for refreshments and a path with steep steps that led from the garden down to the river bank. Stables were to one side of the hostelry and a horse trough stood at the front under three towering elm trees. The whole site was demolished in 1876 when Lambeth Waterworks bought the land for low-level reservoirs. The pub moved to Portsmouth Road next to Windmill Lane.

Three Pigeons

The Three Pigeons at its 'new' site in Portsmouth Road.

THE Three Pigeons served ales to the working class of Long Ditton for at least 150 years. It was originally on the river side of Portsmouth Road, below road level, near today's marina, and had a spring in the garden. The site was acquired by the water board in Victorian times and the hostelry was relocated across the road next to Prospect Place. It was pulled down in the late 1970s and the site was used for car showrooms.

In 1839, the coaching inn was listed as simply the Pigeons, and a woman ran it. Many Portsmouth-bound waggons and horses were kept here overnight for long journeys. By 1855, the landlord was William Ayling. In the above picture, at the 'new' site, W Abbott was the keeper.

The 'Pigeons' at the same site before demolition in 1978.

Chickens strut in road

Winters Bridge

LONG before trams arrived at Winters (Window's) Bridge in 1906, the little community on both sides of the Portsmouth road was a busy one.

Coaching inns were plentiful here and some of the customers would have been the workmen employed on the wharfs.

The ancient Claremont Wharf was so named because it was here that heavy bulk items destined for the new Claremont House at Esher in the 18th century were unloaded from the river's cargo carriers and taken the remaining short journey by road.

A wharf has existed at this location for centuries and, apart from a spot near Walton, is the most southerly point of the Thames.

Claremont Wharf became the distribution point for the coal merchant business of the Styles family whose name is synonymous with Long Ditton.

Forde Farm estate behind the Winters Bridge shops on the Thames Ditton side was expanded in 1763 by the wealthy owner, Charlotte Digby. The new area ran along the river to the City Arms and took in Claremont Wharf. She had purchased the land from the Hatton family.

However, she sold the land in 1786 to Charlotte Boyle Walsingham who had the farm buildings pulled down and a palatial building erected. She named her new home Boyle Farm.

From the old Three Pigeons on the river side of the Portsmouth

Chickens strut around the middle of the Portsmouth Road in late Victorian times. A horse-drawn carriage has pulled up outside the Mason's Arms and pedestrians walk leisurely down the centre of the highway without fear of being run over. It was some years before the tram lines were laid here.

Road to the Kingston boundary were osier beds and meadows stretching along the river bank. Just across the boundary was the original Fox and Hounds pub at Seething Wells, demolished in 1856 for waterworks expansion.

It was here, in the Fox and Hounds' garden, where the bubbling spring which gave the locality its name could be found. On early maps, it is shown as Siden Wells. The well house was covered with ivy.

A Surbiton photographer, George William Ayliffe, who traded in Brighton Road, Surbiton until his retirement in 1885, related his memories of the district to the *Surrey Comet* just before the First World War. In these articles, he recalls life in the 1840s and 1850s. Reminiscing about Winters Bridge, he said there were cottages where the Mason's Arms was later built. Looking from this spot towards Surbiton, he said that beyond these cottages, there were only meadows and ploughed fields all the way to the Brighton Road which was then known as the

Kingston-Leatherhead Turnpike. The only exception was a large house, The Cedars, set near to the road just beyond the Crown and Anchor, with a fine view across the river towards Hampton Court Palace. The four acres of grounds behind the house — mainly lawns — and the two fields beyond were used each year for the Dittons Horticultural and Industrial Society Annual Show. This was before the water companies had extended their operation to Windmill Lane.

A country scene in Rectory Lane, before motor vehicles became the usual mode of transport.

Recollections of rustic scenes in Rectory Lane

A FASCINATING insight into the life and times of Long Ditton at the beginning of the 1900s has been made possible by Charles Douglas 'Jack' Mason, a former resident, who wrote his delightful memories down on paper in retirement.

Jack arrived in Long Ditton in 1900 at the age of three weeks. His father had secured a job as coachman at Saxonbury, a large mansion in St Mary's Road, opposite and just downhill from Cockcrow Hill. His father worked for the mansion owner, Mrs George Bowring. Jack's grandfather was employed by Hartmanns at Newlands, Thames Ditton.

Jack Mason lived at the Saxonbury coachhouse for 20 years, until 1920, when the family moved away. He became a Surbiton solicitor.

Throughout this book, some of Jack's vivid descriptions of Long Ditton have been incorporated.

These two charming photographs portray how much of Upper Long Ditton at the end of the 19th century was a tranquil, rural corner of Surrey, then untouched by developers. A few large houses with acres of grounds and a few cottages were all that there was to be found.

Rectory Lane was earlier known as Watery Lane owing to downhill trickle from the Manor House. Jack Mason wrote that there were no buildings in Rectory Lane apart from Old Gunner's Cottage and the Rectory. He recalls his uncle, William Mason, saying how a hunt once came down the lane and a stag jumped the Rectory's five-bar gate.

Plough and Harrow — and an alleged scandal at the Surrey Cycle Works

IMAGINE if walls could talk. The Plough and Harrow's would have the most tales to tell. For generations, this public house in Ditton Hill Road has been host to countless visits by villagers either wanting to celebrate, have a quiet chat, or drink until they are merry.

The building above was pulled down in 1930 and rebuilt. On the left is Walter W Perkis's Surrey Cycle Works. Pictured to the right of this picture, taken circa1905, is a garage. By 1943, Fred Marty was the proprietor and remained so for decades

after. Also next to the pub's forecourt was the little fire station.

The pub has seen some memorable incidents over the years including the time some drunken men brought a pony, which had earlier been purchased in Tolworth, into the bar. The landlord was enraged.

For a good many years, Walter William Perkis ran the Surrey Cycle Works. In March 1908 he hit the headlines of the Sunday papers for an alleged scandal.

It was reported that Kingston county justices heard a case claiming that Mr Perkis was the father of an illegitimate child. It was said he advertised in a religious paper for a housekeeper, stating he was a widower. Mr Perkis, of Chestnut Villas, Ditton Hill, as a result took on Margaret Ellen Twine, a widow, of Tolworth, who claimed she had given birth to Mr Perkis's child while in his employment in 1906. Mr Perkis, it transpired, was still married and Mrs Twine was demanding maintenance, which

Mr Perkis had refused to pay. "After intimacy in the bedroom after a few days in his employment, she became in a certain condition," the court was told.

He had ensured the male child was delivered "without a nurse, a medical man, or medical attendance of any kind whatever."

The complainant wore a dress of mixed cloth, with a white fur boa and a hat of black lace as she gave evidence. Perkis denied it all.

The summons was dismissed.

End of an era for horse-drawn buses

THE railway had put paid to the stage-coach and now the coming of the electric trams had forced the horse-drawn buses off the road.

In April 1906, the *Surrey Comet* asked: "Who would have thought 16 to 20 years ago — when the first one-horsed omnibus ran from Kingston to Surbiton — that they would be rendered useless by the swift-running electric cars?

"Yet the slowness of the bidding at the Three Pigeons Hotel, Long Ditton, on Monday when Mr A Smelt put up for auction the rolling stock and horses which had recently been running on the Kingston to Esher route, must have convinced the observer that omnibuses are becoming a drug in the market.

"In spite of two alluring announcements that they could be 'admirably adapted for motor power', three out of the four vehicles were bought at absurdly low prices; two being knocked down at five guineas and one at four guineas.

"Then, one by one, the 17 horses were led out before the critical gaze of their audience. Some bore an air of having resigned themselves to the inevitable, while others strongly objected to the indignity and surveyed the crowd with a haughty stare. In most cases they had to be content with a buyer at between eight and ten guineas, but a look of pained surprise was to be observed on the faces of 'Ginger' and 'Jane' when they were knocked down at four guineas each."

A horse-drawn bus to Esher leaves Kingston in 1904 – two years before electric trams to the Dittons 'rendered them useless'.

LONDON UNITED ELECTRIC TRAMWAYS.

THE UNDERMENTIONED LINES OF THE

SURREY EXTENSION

OF THE COMPANY'S SYSTEM

ARE NOW OPEN

FOR PUBLIC TRAFFIC.

Cars Run in accordance with the following

TIME TABLE :—

RICHMOND BRIDGE & WINDOW'S BRIDGE LINE.

The First Car will leave RICHMOND BRIDGE at 7.45 a.m. and at intervals of Ten minutes until 9.55 p.m.; then at 10.15 p.m., 10.40 p.m., and every Twenty minutes until 11.20 p.m.

The First Car will leave WINDOW'S BRIDGE at 7.15 a.m.; then at 7.30 and 7.45 a.m., and every Ten minutes until 8.55 p.m.; then at 9.15 p.m., 9.40 p.m. and every Twenty minutes until 10.40 p.m., and at 10.51 p.m. (Cars will then continue running until 12.30 midnight to Fulwell Depot (Teddington) only.

KINGSTON HILL & WINDOW'S BRIDGE LINE.

The First Car will leave KINGSTON HILL at 7.30 a.m.; and at intervals of Ten minutes until 9.0 p.m.; then every Twenty minutes until 11.20 p.m. after which cars will continue running until 12.0 midnight to Fulwell Depot (Teddington) only.

The First Car will leave WINDOW'S BRIDGE at 7.40 a.m.; and at intervals of Ten minutes until 9.30 p.m.; then every Twenty minutes until 11.20 p.m.

KINGSTON HILL & HAMPTON COURT LINE.

The First Car will leave KINGSTON HILL at 7.35 a.m.; and at intervals of Ten minutes until 9.55 p.m.; then at 10.10 p.m. and every twenty minutes until 11.30 p.m. Cars will then continue running until 12.0 midnight to Fulwell Depot (Teddington) only.

The First Car will leave HAMPTON COURT at 8.0 a.m.; and at intervals of Ten minutes until 9.40 p.m.; then every twenty minutes until 11.20 p.m.

SURBITON STATION & EWELL ROAD (TOLWORTH) LINE.

The First Car will leave SURBITON STATION at 7.20 a.m.; and at intervals of Five minutes until 9.30 p.m.; and then every Ten minutes until 11.50 p.m.

The First Car will leave EWELL ROAD (Tolworth) at 7.30 a.m.; and at intervals of Five minutes until 9.40 p.m.; and then every Ten minutes until 12.0 midnight.

Announcements in the Surrey Comet of Saturday 3rd March 1906, giving details of the two new electric tramcar services from Long Ditton (Window's Bridge). Services ran every 10 minutes to both Kingston Hill and Richmond.

FARES.

RICHMOND BRIDGE & WINDOW'S BRIDGE (LONG DITTON)

Richmond Bridge and Junction of Stanley and Hampton Roads (Twickenham)	
London Road and York Street (Twickenham) and Wesleyan Chapel, Broad Street (Teddington)	
Junction of Stanley and Hampton Roads (Twickenham) and St. Alban's Church (Teddington)	1D
Wesleyan Chapel, Broad Street (Teddington) and Kingston Bridge	
Kingston Bridge and Surbiton Railway Station	
Surbiton Railway Station and Window's Bridge (Long Ditton)	
Richmond Bridge and St. Alban's Church (Teddington)	
Junction of London Road & York Street (Twickenham) and Kingston Bridge	2D
Wesleyan Chapel, Broad Street (Teddington) and Surbiton Railway Station	
Kingston Bridge and Window's Bridge (Long Ditton)	
Richmond Bridge and Kingston Bridge	
London Road and York Street (Twickenham) and Surbiton Railway Station	3D
Wesleyan Chapel, Broad Street (Teddington) & Window's Bridge (Long Ditton)	
Richmond Bridge and Surbiton Railway Station	
London Road and York Street (Twickenham) and Window's Bridge (Long Ditton)	4D
Richmond Bridge and Window's Bridge (Long Ditton)	5D

KINGSTON HILL & WINDOW'S BRIDGE (LONG DITTON)

Kingston Hill and Surbiton Railway Station	
Surbiton Railway Station and Window's Bridge (Long Ditton)	1D
Kingston Hill and Window's Bridge (Long Ditton)	2D

The Mason's Arms was an old coaching inn on the Portsmouth Road. The public house's livery and bait stables, offering open and closed carriages, stands next door fronting Thorkhill Road. The pub became Billy Bunters in the 1980s and later Green's Brasserie.

The muddy tram terminus at Winters Bridge in about 1906. The Masons Arms is on the right. Its next-door neighbour was a butcher.

Ticket to Window's Bridge

HORSE-DRAWN buses, tramcars, trolleybuses, RF single-deckers — and then 'hoppas' for shoppers — Long Ditton has seen them all. The village has been privileged to witness some of the most exciting eras in the history of public road transport.

Trams first arrived at Winters Bridge — or Window's Bridge as the destination boards later proclaimed after complaints about the mis-spelling — on 1st March 1906.

London United Tramways' managing director, James Clifton Robinson, born 1848, had sampled trams on both sides of the Atlantic and was set on introducing them in south London. His enthusiasm saw the project through, despite public fears. He was knighted in 1905 and a year later, the trams commenced in Surbiton, Kingston and the Dittons where three new services

operated. A gang of 50 men had put up the cables and a further 100 had laid the tracks in the region.

On the first day of operation Sir Clifton was injured when a tram collided with a Hodgson's Kingston brewery carriage dray at Kingston Hill. He fell onto his back in the road.

The Dittons tram ran initially to Kingston Hill — the George and Dragon — but two months later, open-topped trams covered a route to Richmond Bridge via Twickenham.

By 1908, the route had apparently been trimmed back to Kingston Hill, at least for a time.

On the Sunday evening of 6th July 1913, Miss Agnes Gray of 4 Cholmley Villas was alighting from a tramcar at the terminus when she slipped and fell. She was conveyed to Thames Ditton Cottage Hospital where she was detained, suffering from shock and injuries to her back.

DOWN	Fare	UP
Wesleyan Chapel	1½d	Richm'nd Bridge
St Alban's Church		Twicken-h'm
Bushey Park Rd.		St Jn.
Hampton Wick Stn		Twicken-ham Gn.
Kingston (Eden St. Junction)		Stanley Rd. Junc
Surbiton Park Ter		Wesleyan Chapel
Surbiton Station		St Alban's Church
Water-works Cr.		Bushey Park Rd.
The Dittons		Hampton Wick Stn.
		Kingston (Eden St. Junc.)

London United Tramways, Ltd.

A Dittons to Richmond Bridge tram ticket. On the reverse of the ticket is an advert for Holloway's Ointment — the all-round remedy.

PORTSMOUTH ROAD, SURBITON.

Long Ditton Post Office, above, traded at Cholmley Terrace, Winters Bridge, from Victorian times to 1st October 1977. The Page family ran the business when this Edwardian photograph was taken.

Pictured beneath, a tram negotiates the tricky turn outside The Globe pub at the junction of Portsmouth Road and Brighton Road.

The 73 tram at Winters Bridge

In 1912, The Dittons tram service was given a number — the 73 — after London United Tramways merged with a Middlesex tram firm. Within four years of this photograph being taken on 30th November 1929, the tram service had been replaced by trolleybuses.

Childhood memories of the 'haunted' old Rectory

RECTOR'S daughter Patsie Wilson was only 11 years when she left the old Rectory in Long Ditton but her schoolgirl recollections of the lovely old building stayed with her forever.

Patsie was born at the Rectory in 1924 and she left in 1937 when the historic house was sold. In later life she recalled fondly: "I realise that no one could have spent a happier childhood in more perfect surroundings."

Patsie wrote: "Going through the gates on the road, the house could be seen standing back on the right. One approached the house by the drive, which circled round a magnificent fir tree, and on the left of the gate, the drive went directly to the stables, which we used as a garage.

I remember the stables were inhabited by a large white barn owl which used to appear at night-time.

Before entering the house, one's attention was drawn to an old stone block, which in past times was used for mounting horses.

As one entered the house, there was a small entrance hall, leading to a much larger hall, which had a staircase on the left side. Immediately to the left, there was a long passageway and my father's study was on the right. This was a lovely long room, with a low ceiling, and bookcases on every wall.

At the end of the passage there was a large drawing room that had been built in Victorian times. The passages in the Elizabethan part of the house all faced south, and the rooms faced north, which seemed the practice in those days, as they wished to avoid sunlight.

At the far end of the hall, a wide passageway led to the dining room and from this passage one could enter the garden through French windows.

Going back to the entrance hall, on the immediate right, my father had a large and untidy work room, and at the far end of this there was a cloakroom on one side and a door leading to the kitchen quarters on the other. The kitchen could also be approached direct from the entrance hall.

The kitchen quarters were very dismal and dark, with an old black range in the kitchen and a pantry and scullery leading off. There was an old-fashioned bread oven in this part and a hand pump on the wall to draw water. There were also large cellars beneath the kitchen.

Rev James Roydon Hughes was Rector of Long Ditton in late Victorian times — between 1874 and 1889.

Leading from the scullery there was a back door, which brought one to an old stone courtyard surrounded by numerous outbuildings and a granary. This was a wonderful place to play in and I remember the roof came down fairly low in this part and we could climb all over the houses from there.

Going up the staircase in the main hall, one came to a long passage on the right, similar to the one below. There was a large bedroom on the right known as a the night nursery. At the far end, in the Victorian part, there

Inside the hallway of the old Rectory.

Long Ditton Rectory and the driveway which encircled "a magnificent fir tree".

were two bedrooms with a dressing room in the middle.

In the opposite direction, there was an interesting room on the left, which we kept for visitors. It had some valuable stained glass in the windows. We had been told that Oliver Cromwell had slept there on one occasion. As the room was over the kitchen, and slightly warmer than the others, we used to have it as a sick room. Once, when I was recovering from at attack of measles, I told my mother that I had seen "a funny little man" come into my room in the night, and I described someone perfectly in Puritan dress.

Continuing down the passage from the spare room, there was a bathroom on the right and a day nursery next to it. We spent a great deal of time in this room, as it was always warm.

Opposite the day nursery there was a very spacious airing cupboard and from that room we could climb right up under the eaves and explore above nearly all the rooms in the old part.

There was another long passage leading to two maids' rooms, then up a few stairs to two further rooms which we used as a playroom and boxroom. I never liked going down there at night, or using the back staircase as it was supposed to be haunted.

The garden always seemed to be beautifully kept, as we had a wonderful gardener called Peter, who worked for us full-time.

If one approached the garden from the door in the hall passageway, one came to the lawn, which had a beautiful oak tree in one corner. Beyond the lawn there was a flower and vegetable garden, surrounded by a high brick wall, and stretching half way down the road. At the far end there was a small coppice of evergreens.

By the Victorian part of the house there was another lawn, with many evergreens on one side and a nut walk on the other. This led to a very old summer house. Beside this, there was a gate to the fields. These fields were a great joy to us, as we had endless games in them. In one corner was a large mound with several trees growing on it. It was known as the Castle.

Beyond this other lawn was a pond, and in this area we kept our chickens.

There were many stables and barns built in Elizabethan times.

My mother told me that the old parishioners remembered Queen Victoria driving past the house, as apparently this used to be one of her favourite drives.

It seems such a tragedy that Long Ditton Rectory no longer

The Rectory pond. Chickens were kept nearby.

The Rectory's centuries-old summer house.

exists, but when my father sold it, it was, I understand, with the assurance that it would be preserved for all time.

When the house was pulled down, the workmen found a walled-up room for which there was no explanation."

Staves used to mark Long Ditton boundary
Beating the bounds

ANCIENT custom in parishes was to mark the boundaries each year. Churchwardens would hold up staves and drop them vertically at the spot where the boundary lines fell. This was fine when the area was fields but increasingly difficult as the area became developed. Below, St Mary's rector, Rev John Harvey, holds a ceremony just after the Second World War at the end of Ferry Road, Long Ditton. A prayer would have been said and a hymn sung. Historically, any encroachment of the parish from neighbours would have been reported to the powers that be.

The ferry took people to and from the landing stage at the bottom of Ferry Road, Long Ditton, to Home Park on the Middlesex banks. The fare was one penny for many years.

Rev John Harvey at the Ferry Road ceremony.

A boy with a goods-laden cart stops on a sunny spring morning to talk to a villager at Bates cottages at the foot of Ditton Hill, c1905. Long Ditton's name probably means "farm by the dike or ditch". Early names include "Ditune" in 1086 and "Longa Dittone" in 1242.

Ditton Hill crossroads

THIS charming picture shows the crossroads at Ditton Hill in about 1905. St Mary's Road is on the right and Church Road and Bates Cottages on the left.

Dating back to at least early Victorian times, these cottages were made into one large home to house Belgian women refugees during the First World War, before their eventual demolition. A war memorial and gardens were created on the site.

Today, the gardens are a pleasant spot, but in the 1950s, the view was of the overgrown gardens of Chalcott House where poor people lived in almost slum conditions. And across the road, some people dumped their rubbish on the grass verge.

The picket fence in the foreground, left, surrounded the front garden of Ditton Hill post office. The post office part of the shop traded here by 1st July 1895 and the business transferred to 45 Fleece Road, further down the road, in the 1930s.

Bates Cottages were home in the late Victorian period to villagers such as George Colman, Thomas Dean, William Spittels, and William Eves. Mr Dean lived there from about 1885 to 1912.

The old post office, Ditton Hill, in about 1906. Once it was an overflow schoolroom for a workhouse next door. St Mary's Church owned the post office for many years. Oscar-winning film director John Bryan lived here between 1947 and 1954.

'Upper Long Ditton' and 'Ditton Hill'

Old post offices

DITTON Hill's first post office, 'Upper Long Ditton' was trading by 1855 at The Farmhouse (much later renamed The Cottage — Long Ditton's oldest standing building in 1998). Nathaniel Holder ran the business for some 15 years. By 1895, and probably earlier, the PO had moved to the old house on the opposite side of the road. Here, as "Ditton Hill PO" it remained until its transfer to the corner of Fleece Road and Ditton Hill Road in about 1935.

In the early 1900s, the post office and stores at Ditton Hill was the only shop in the Ditton Hill area. Fleece Road parade was not built until 1908. From 1917 to 1935 a Mrs White ran the PO. Young boys used to bang on her door when closed to ask for Players cigarettes for their fathers. Mrs White came from a family brought to the village by Rector Alfred Martell from his previous parish at Petersfield to work as his domestic staff at the Rectory.

This postcard was mailed at 'Upper Long Ditton' post office in March 1889. It was posted by Charles Lavers-Smith who had just moved into Woodstock, Woodstock Lane. He died aged 87 and had become a prominent figure in the local community. The 'new' post office was renamed Ditton Hill and here it stayed until c1935 after which it became a house.

A winter's day at Ditton Hill more than a century ago. The entrance drive to the house, Cumbrae, is on the right.

Ditton men's char-a-banc trip to seaside

THERE are no ladies present in this men only outing to Brighton seafront. The photograph, taken in the early part of the 1900s, captures several of Long Ditton's bygone characters.

They include Bill Smithers, from Kings Road, a printer; Harry Freeman, of the Rushett, a builder; 'Tiger' Foster, a bricklayer; 'Smiler' Harding, a groundsman; 'Piggy' White, who worked for St Mary's church and whose family lived above the old post office, Ditton Hill; Nobby Warren and farmhand, Albert Rainbow, of Jasmine Cottage, Summerfield Lane.

Also pictured in the char-a-banc, an early type of long open coach, were Walter Tilley, a driver with Hawk's ginger beer company at Thames Ditton; Curley Irwin, a bricklayer; Charlie Smithers — "a quiet, tidy man"; Mr Smith, a gardener; Mr Goulder, of South Bank, who worked for Gosworth's; Perce Bracey, who worked as a railway inspector; Mr Beer, and Mr Hammond.

In 1921, the year Rev Robert Wilson took over as rector, the population of Long Ditton was 2,976.

By 1925, the population had exceeded 3,000 and the little village as it was in earlier times was rapidly being replaced by a busier, rather more suburban community.

The Kingston bypass was under construction and soon, many fields around Hinchley Wood would be covered in concrete as fashionable housing estates were constructed close to the new arterial road. However, there were still many unspoilt corners of Long Ditton which retained their rural charm. In 1925, none of the houses in Ewell Road had yet been built, the police station was still open at Ferry Road and the little fire station continued to provide a valuable service next to the Plough and Harrow, Ditton Hill Road.

Along the Portsmouth Road, there was a hive of industrial activity, as there had been for very many years.

Thomas Styles continued to trade — after several decades — as a coal merchant and lighterman at Claremont Wharf, next to the River Thames; Mr E J Newns ran a motor garage at City Wharf nearby, and George Page sold sweets and ran the Long Ditton post office and telephone call office at Cholmley Terrace.

Of the few private telephones in the parish at this time, one was at the Mason Engineering Company, next to the Mason's Arms — Kingston 370; and another was at John and David Lang's at Manor Farm, Woodstock Lane, Claygate — Esher 148.

In the Fleece Road shopping parade, between Ditton Hill Road and Rectory Lane were, in order, Mrs L S Murrell's cash provision stores; John Smith's fishmonger's; Mrs A Harman's sweet shop; James Gammon, the window cleaner's; Mrs Mary Boakes' wardrobe dealer's; Mrs King's and George Watson's premises; Alfred Burton's butcher's; George Curtis and William Hampshire's premises; William Wright's boot repairer's; Fred Thorne's hairdresser's salon and Mrs M Ritchley's store.

At the Rushett, the little shops in the terraces had gone, but James Bailey, of The Orchard, was a tree lopper, Fred Fenn, of 1 Gloucester Cotts, made watches; Fred Mathews and Wallace Mills were builders and Samuel Sawyer at 4 Rushett Terrace was a French polisher. George Thurkettle ran the Rushett hand laundry.

Bygone landlords of the Plough and Harrow

Regulars arrive on horseback at the old Plough and Harrow shortly before the pub was rebuilt in 1930. To the right is a garage which, from 1943 to recent times, was run by Fred Marty. After a few drinks, a local sweep used to wobble his way home by bicycle with the rain forming sooty black rivulets of water down his face.

E. Hassell, who painted many Surrey scenes in the 1830s, captured the Plough and Harrow on a visit.

OLD maps of 1793 show the Plough and Harrow being an ancient thatched building. At this time, Ditton Hill Road was also known as Long Ditton Street or Long Ditton Hill.

Only a handful of isolated cottages and farms, along with the Rectory, the church and the Manor House existed in the village at this time.

By 1839, Evan Caslett was running the pub and appears to have been landlord for around 10 years, being succeeded in 1850 by his widow, Mary, for a year after his death at the age of 62.

The following 18 years, until about 1873, the drinking house was in the hands of William Welham. For a decade up to 1889, William Coslett ran the establishment. John Burgess took over in 1890 for a year before the business went firstly to Mr Loveland, then William Aspen, and in 1898, to Joseph Smith until 1909. Mrs Amy Campbell ran it for two years until 1912, being succeeded by Samuel Smith until 1925. Mrs C Smith was landlady up to about 1930.

Groups of men could become quite high-spirited after a few drinks. On one occasion, some local gents thought it bad form that the pub did not have a Christmas tree one yuletide. They uprooted a tree from outside and dragged it into the bar, finding the whole episode the source of much mirth.

In the final few years of the 20th century, Kim and Gerry Stone were in charge. They helped to ensure the continuance of the pub's strong sense of community by organising many charity events.

Some of the old pub ways have long since vanished. Barbecues, bouncy castles, children's pets and evening meals have taken their place as the venue, along with others across the land, attempts to cater for the the needs of families as well as the regular male drinkers of the type who frequented bars in in the past.

Long Ditton fire station

A RED wooden and corrugated iron fire station once stood to the left of the Plough and Harrow's front entrance by Perkis's Surrey Cycle Works. The Dittons and Claygate Fire Brigade was formed in 1882 and it had a horse-drawn pump at Watts Road, Thames Ditton, and a hose reel appliance at Long Ditton. Of the brigade's nine firemen, two were based at Ditton Hill Road. In 1896, the local service merged with the Esher Fire Brigade to form the Esher and The Dittons Urban District Fire Brigade.

By 1911, Thomas Dean was foreman at Long Ditton — station no 3 in the Esher and Dittons Brigade — and in 1924, he became station officer. He lived in the Old School House next door.

The fire station appears to have been decommissioned in 1930 and demolished along with the former Plough and Harrow. Number 66 Ditton Hill Road is roughly where the station was situated.

Albert Rainbow mows the fields behind the old Rectory in Long Ditton. The fields, some kept by a Mr Scott, sloped down to Sugden Road. The only property between Rectory Lane and the Surbiton Sports Club ground was a solitary cottage with bow windows.

Upper Ditton House and gardens

Upper Ditton House — home of a royal gardener.

UPPER Ditton House, or 'Long Ditton House' stood in the middle of the village where the infants school was built in 1910-1911. It was set in nine acres of beautiful gardens, paddocks and meadows. Just across the road was the old Plough and Harrow.

It was no doubt a brick house but the bricks were probably covered with white stucco. A flight of steps led up to the front door which had pillars each side, supporting a porch with a flat roof. All around the roof were battlements. A remarkable panel on the outside of the house depicted Greeks and Amazons in furious combat.

Of the garden, it was said, "nothing could state its infinite variety". There were two lawns, with beds of formal cut, and a very large oval field, round the whole of which was a broad path with laurels and rhododendrons and all kinds of shrubs and flowering trees on either side. There was also a wilderness left alone to do as it pleased. Here, the high trees almost shut out the sky. The house was built in the late 17th century for royal gardener George London and rebuilt in the late 18th century. There were then fields on both sides of Fleece Road — in the early 1840s known as Occupation Road. The area that became Ditton Hill Terrace (nicknamed Marmalade Terrace) and Kings Road were also green open spaces. MP Thomas Smith lived at the house in the 1880s.

The modern houses built opposite the Plough and Harrow were constructed on the land used for the house's kitchen gardens— "a place shut in by red brick walls with a high iron gate which was always locked". Upper Ditton House was bounded by large areas of land belonging to the Earl of Lovelace, landlord of many of Long Ditton's sprawling acres.

The Grange, St Mary's Road — home to a wealthy churchwarden.

The Grange, St Mary's Road

THE Grange stood in three and a half acres of gardens in St Mary's Road, next door to Hillside, home of the Clayton family for some 80 years. By 1895, the Grange was the home of Robert Jackson Bates. He was a churchwarden at St Mary's and was described as "wealthy and generous". To the rear was Cockcrow Hill and the spacious Southborough Park.

In 1822, Long Ditton rector Rev Bryan Broughton took a walk to Cockcrow Hill one spring morning and wrote a poem after stopping to admire the panoramic views. Then there was hardly a building in sight — the nearest neighbours included Pound Farm in the valley and Hill Farm on top of Ditton Hill. Before him were miles of rolling fields. He was so mesmerised by the beauty he stayed until midday and penned "Copse Grove Hill", or "Reflections made in a Spring Morning at Sunrise on its Summit in the Parish of Long Ditton Surry, 1822". The poem stretches to 25 pages.

The Grange survived as flats until 1979.

An early photo, said to have been taken at the time of the Crimean war (1853-6) at Bates Cottages, Ditton Hill, showing Fred and Charlie Brooks from a family whose business was saddles.

Most villagers did not own a bath

New parish hall plan

WHEN the Industrial Revolution hit Britain, much of agricultural Long Ditton was unaffected. But along the river, the waterworks arrived in the 1850s and its staff moved into rows of houses built along Winters Road, Howard Road and Prospect Place. Across the Portsmouth Road, businesses thrived along the water's edge at Claremont and City Wharfs. Later Fred Styles' coal yard added to the hive of activity in the locality.

The large influx of working-class men and their families put pressure on local facilities. And the menfolk in particu-

Plans for a new hall and details of a fund-raising appeal to pay for it were described in a 1906 leaflet.

The first parish room, built 1888 at Thorkhill Road, with a corrugated iron hall at the rear. The latter was to be demolished by a flying bomb in June 1944 along with gym equipment inside.

lar wanted somewhere to meet socially, other than at Swan Cottage in Portsmouth Road, where they had congregated since 1833. The Chelsea Waterworks men met in the Balaclava Hall in Balaclava Road, Surbiton, opposite today's Surbiton Baptist Church. The church also used the little hall when it was formed in June 1898.

Eventually, funds were raised to build the large parish hall at the corner of Thorkhill Road and Ewell Road, Long Ditton, in 1888.

The hall became the hub of village social life — and it was somewhere in late Victorian times where parishioners could take a bath. Nine out of 10 households in this area did not possess a bath.

By 1900, it had become obvious that the hall was not large enough to meet the needs of Long Ditton's expanding population and a fund-raising appeal was launched to provide a new hall alongside the old parish room.

Land was purchased for £200 on which to construct the 74ft long hall.

It was intended that the hall would be able to seat 460 people and have a platform for private parties, concerts and other entertainments as well as serving as a venue for "evening services, Bible classes, Band of Hope meetings and cookery classes." The project was expected to cost more than £2,000.

The hall's trustees included the Rector, Rev Charles Hughes; Charles H Clayton, of Hillside, St Mary's Road; C Denny; W H Hutchinson; W Stevenson of Eaglehurst, St Mary's Road; G B Windeler and A W Cousins. The new hall opened in 1907.

One of the chief fund-raisers had been Mrs 'Willie' Stevenson of Eaglehurst. She opened up her garden in the summer of 1905 and collected £500.

The event was blessed with beautiful weather and the *Surrey Comet* wrote: "A more ideal spot for such a function it would be difficult to find; the four lawns providing ample accommodation for the marquees and at the same time affording excellent opportunities for games of various kinds. The weather was as ideal as the surroundings. The fierce rays of the Midsummer sun being tempered by a refreshing breeze. Best of all the attendance was large and fashionable; the cream of local society being present."

Gold and silver pheasants in the grounds

Chalcott House and Nellie in the stables

Miss Trouncer converted Chalcott House's stables (above) into a beautiful country cottage (below).

ONE of Ditton Hill's most colourful characters was Nellie Trouncer, a likeable Surbiton spinster who spent her final years in the stable block of Chalcott House, which she converted into one of the prettiest cottages around.

Describing herself as "terribly shy and silly" and "so afraid of being laughed at, I gave up asking questions and bottled everything up", she was the daughter of a Surbiton doctor.

The family had moved firstly to Ditton Hill and soon became acquainted with well-known Ditton families of the day: the Perkins, Bathos, Claytons, Reusses, Stevensons, Bulmer Howells, Wimbles, Cavendishes and Bates. Of Percy Bates she wrote: "Ask anyone if they know a more energetic man than Percy, the father. If he were anywhere about, the only way was to hide or be completely worn out. Even on Sundays he would sing in the choir, remove his cassock and dash down the aisle to collect; it being doubtful if he could get back to the choir in time for the last verse of the hymn."

Born in 1869, Nellie was in her mid forties when she arrived in 1915 at Chalcott House, which her brother, Harold, was to buy from the Lovelace estate in 1929. Her conversion of the stables into a picture-postcard home drew admiration from many and she was praised for the lovely walled garden which has remained unspoilt, even in modern times.

Chalcott House "in Long Ditton Street" dated back to about 1835 and in 1857, Lady Harriet Catherine Wegg Prosser became a tenant. The house at that time had gardens, orchards and three acres and the yearly rent from the Lovelace

Miss Trouncer — "terribly silly and shy" — lived at Littlecot, (82 and 82a) Ditton Hill Road.

estate was 3/8d. Mrs Wegg Prosser died in 1893 and left it to her husband, Francis. When he died, it went to their second son, Charles Edward, who lived until 1925. In September 1918, Harold Trouncer bought for £500 the freehold of one and a half acres of land at the corner of Rectory Lane and Church Road, just up from Chalcott House. The house, gardens and outbuildings he purchased in 1929 for £3,560. Then, in 1936, Mr Trouncer sold the house, former stables (Littlecot), outbuildings and gardens to the Ditton Hill Investment Trust for £4,650. The trust sold the estate to Hygienic Homes for £3,500 in 1946 and the same year, Littlecot became the property of Herbert John Hickman.

In the war, Chalcott House was used to house evacuated children from East London. By 1948 it was converted to seven flats but not long after became in a poor state of repair and was pulled

down about 1961.

Local children liked to play in the ruins of the grand old house.

Another of the old mansion's occupiers many years ago was Colonel Charles Freville Surtees, a Conservative MP for South Durham between 1865 and 1868. He lived at the house from 1862 for 30 years and served with the 10th Hussars.

His grounds were said to have been full of gold and silver pheasants. He died in 1906 and is buried in Long Ditton.

In 1936, Miss Trouncer published a book called *An Old Fashioned Miss* which is packed with amusing, humorous recollections of her life.

In one chapter, she recalls how she was picking pears in the garden of Littlecot, standing on high steps when she fell because her basket was too heavy. "Not having a maid living in, I thought 'whatever happens, I must get help or I shall be here all night'." When eventually a doctor arrived, he tried to cut the casualty's dress off but she refused to let him.

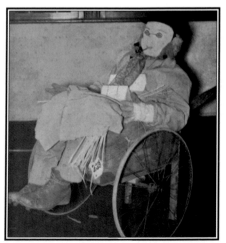

Nellie Trouncer, a keen amateur actress, was behind this disguise which bemused a Surrey Comet photographer.

Schoolhouse, Ditton Hill

LONG Ditton appears to have had no school in medieval times. Even as late as 1725, when the Bishop of Winchester visited the village, he wrote that there was "no school in the parish".

Local historian Peter Fussell, who in retirement researched the education of children in Long Ditton as part of a general probe into the area's past, noted that it was quite usual in the 18th century for there not to be a school in Britain's small towns and villages.

He explained that in 1811 the National Society was set up with the rather pompous name, The National Society for Promoting the Education of the Poor in the Principles of the Established Church. Later, under this scheme, Long Ditton had a "National School". It is certainly listed as such in 1840.

The school only had a few pupils and was held in a small cottage in what is now known as Ditton Hill Road. Before its demolition in about 1930, it stood where the back gardens of numbers 76 and 78 Ditton Hill Road are situated today.

A map of 1865 shows the cottage standing on its own at the end of a curved driveway — now 74 Ditton Hill Road. At the back of the school was a tree-lined field of more than two acres beyond which was Watery Lane (Rectory Lane) and the Tudor Rectory.

THE OLD SCHOOLHOUSE. DITTON HILL SURREY.   D32

The former National School which stood at the rear of 76 and 78 Ditton Hill Road. Pupils were taught for a penny a week.

The 'new' school at the Rushett after completion in 1873.

Charles Mason, who lived at the coach house, Saxonbury, St Mary's Road, from 1900 to 1920, once wrote that his father, also Charles, attended the National School and a fee of one penny a week had to be paid for the privilege.

Charles jnr remembered the school was a "very old, ramshackle building". Its nearest next-door neighbours were Chalcott House's little cottages on the upside, and the Plough and Harrow on the downside.

As a boy, Percy Perrin, who for many years lived opposite in Kings Road, recalled a little smallholding between the old schoolhouse and the Plough and Harrow. In the late 1920s, he said, it had a few chickens and was bordered by a white, paling fence. There was a profusion of cow parsley growing on the plot and schoolboys used to pick the cow parsley, let it dry and use the stalks as peashooters. The ammunition came in the form of berries.

In 1881, Charles Spriggs, Hannah Purver and Joseph Martin lived in the old schoolhouse. It was Hannah's home for some 20 years. Nathan Eves was in residence from about 1906 to 1915 and fireman Thomas Dean from the Great War until 1929. For five years another occupant was Charles Florence.

In 1870, Parliament passed the Elementary Education Act to encourage the building of more, and better, schools. In 1872, the Earl of Lovelace gave half an acre of his land at The Rushett to the parish of Long Ditton so that a new larger school could be built.

The Dairy, Winters Bridge

Victorian classrooms

WINTERS Bridge is so named because of a Richard Window who traded as a blacksmith here in the 1770s. At that time, the River Rythe flowed over the main road and this was most inconvenient for the smith's customers. He built a plank bridge to save them from getting their feet wet. The forge, at Thorkhill Road, survived until 1951.

Window's Bridge has been corrupted to Winters Bridge since then and the river has, of course, been culverted under the Portsmouth Road. The Essex Arms, named after the Earls of Essex who owned land in Long Ditton, replaced a dairy at the corner of Ferry Road. The premises also appears to have been a corn chandlers in the past.

In the mid 1980s, new landlords John and Penny Callan re-named the pub The Ferry Tavern. It was originally half the size and regulars used to sit around benches next to open hatches leading to the cellars.

The pub's more recent title recalls the bygone ferry service nearby.

VICTORIAN school life in Long Ditton was often difficult. Classrooms in winter were often so cold that the children cried. Illnesses prevailed and sometimes so many pupils were off, the whole school would have to close.

The village's cottage school by the Plough and Harrow was founded in 1840, but a new education act in 1870 led to the building of the main school at The Rushett in 1873 on land given by the Earl of Lovelace. The cost of the new school was £1,640.

The school had three departments — girls, boys and infants. The first mistress of the infants department was Mrs Sarah Bampton, who, with a pupil-teacher named Fanny Petty, taught reading, writing, singing and marching, arithmetic, needlework, knitting and religion to the 87 children in her charge. Fanny, who earned just £10 per year, may well have been aged just 13 and a former pupil hoping to gain experience for a teacher-training course.

Richard Braddock, from East Harling, became head in August 1875, replacing Mr and Mrs Favelle, who had fallen out with Mrs Hughes, the rector's wife, over an "unbecoming" letter. Mr Braddock's salary was £100 per year with use of the school house. He also had to play the harmonium at church and help with Sunday School.

As Long Ditton's population expanded, infants were transferred to a new department at Ditton Hill Road on 4th September 1911 and remained there for the rest of the 20th century, the school being run by the county council. At the new infants school, there were many problems. Toilets froze up in icy spells, staff were hard to find and two wars had to be endured. The junior school left Rushett for Sugden Road in 1974. The official opening ceremony was conducted by the incumbent Earl of Lovelace on 19th March 1975.

The dairy, Winters Bridge, on the corner of Ferry Road. The old police station, right, is just visible.

Badge of St Mary's School.   *Miss Tranter, head 1940-73.*

Edwardian schooldays

Long Ditton School's class two photographed around 1906.

L ONG Ditton School's log books give a fascinating insight into life in the village in Edwardian times — the period from 1902 to 1910.

Earlier, in 1896, when Queen Victoria was still on the throne, the school in Rushett Road was enlarged. By 1903, the school was almost 30 years old. The following year the master's house was extended and two years later, a new chimney and grate were installed in the infants school at the site.

Up until 1893, the boys and girls were taught separately. Between 1892 and 1905, Mr Munro was the headmaster of firstly the boys' school and then in 1893 he took overall charge of the new, mixed classes until 1905, when Mr Mileham replaced him as head.

The infants section of the school at Rushett Road was headed by Miss Kennett from 1882 to 1904 when Mrs Nettle took charge. She was the last headmistress of the infants department while it was still at Rushett prior to

the children transferring to the new infants school opened at Ditton Hill Road in 1911.

Village children in fancy dress.

Maypole dancing during the Edwardian period which saw some important events in Long Ditton. A new parish hall opened in October 1907 next to the 1888 hall; the Fleece Road shopping parade was built and Kings Road was constructed.

Heavenly holiday home in a railway carriage

Miss Tranter's early years

LONG before coming to Long Ditton school as head-mistress for 32 years, Sybil Tranter had inherited a love of Dorset. And it was here that she spent numerous holidays – in a converted railway carriage — reflecting on the beautiful surroundings which provided the inspiration for her remarkable years working with hundreds of Ditton children between 1941 and 1973.

Miss Tranter was the youngest of Alfred and Fanny Tranter's five children. She was born at Oakfield, 5 St George's Road, Kingston Hill, in 1908. Her father, a former Scots Guard, worked for the Metropolitan Police at Kingston and when he retired from the force, spent some years working for King George V and travelling extensively on royal visits.

Sybil Tranter's mother hailed from Highwood, a tiny Dorset hamlet near Wareham. Her father, from the village of Poxwell near Weymouth. Her grandmother, Mary Tranter, was in mid Victorian times the schoolmistress at Poxwell living in the thatched schoolhouse.

Against this background, a love of Dorset prevailed. As the earlier generations of Tranters passed on, the homes and thatched cottages which had allowed Sybil, her parents and siblings to enjoy so many holidays in this delightful part of the countr passed to new owners.

For Sybil's father, the yearning for a Dorset base to where the family could make return visits grew stronger year by year. Then

Sybil Tranter sitting nearest her father, soon after the railway carriage arrived at the one-acre plot of land at Wool in Dorset. She spent countless holidays in the train house.

Miss Tranter's father and a colleague building a roof over the carriages.

came the opportunity they had waited so long for. Land at Wool became available and Alfred Tranter purchased for £90 exactly one acre on which to build a home.

But it was to be no ordinary house. He and Sybil's mother decided to buy two railway carriages from the Eastleigh depot. They dated back to the 1880s and had been decommissioned. Their last function was to ferry troops in the First World War.

The cost of £35 included delivery to Wool Station sidings, from where they were taken by farm trailer to the field. The antiquated carriages were lovingly restored over the years. A well was dug for water and apple trees and sweet-smelling pinks were planted outside. A roof was put over the carriages and the battleship-grey paintwork was repainted more appropriately.

In the early trips to Dorset, the family would hire a 'fly' to take them from their Kingston home to Surbiton station. This was a type of horse and carriage. The family would then take a train to Dorset.

In 1932, they bought their first car. It was a 1928 Singer saloon. They named it Philomel. Miss Tranter recalled in retirement: "The car had a red triangle fixed to the rear wing to warn other road-users that it had brakes on all four wheels. The engine, alas, was small compared with the large roomy body and it boiled frequently when it struggled to pull its load up the Dorset hills. The family waited patiently by the car until the engine cooled, then they walked to the top of the hill while father followed with the car. It was in this car that the girls learnt to drive. It had no synchromesh gears, so every gear change meant double declutching."

It was on a visit to her beloved train house that Miss Tranter died on 27th May 1997. It was felt this would have been her final wish. A memorial service was later held at Long Ditton. Former deputy head's son Steve Winfield and others paid tributes.

Mr Dymond the caretaker

WILLIAM Dymond was caretaker at Long Ditton School, Rushett Road, for more than a quarter of a century.

From 1920 to 1946, he looked after the Church of England school and got to know hundreds of children and a good number of teachers.

He lived for many years just a short walk away at 6 South Bank, Long Ditton. But Mr Dymond's early life was in sharp contrast to his caretaking job.

As a young man, he served in the Merchant Navy for 29 years and travelled around the world seven times.

Born in Jersey in 1877, his first job at sea was as a steward on the Olympic which sailed from Southampton to Liverpool in June 1912, just two months after the Titanic disaster. Later, he sailed to Australia, New Zealand, Canada, China, and Japan.

For several years, Mr Dymond's wife, Agnes, was a cleaner at Long Ditton School.

The Dymond family's connections with South Bank

William Dymond, caretaker at Long Ditton School, 1920-46.

and social life in the village extended over many years. William and Agnes's son, Frank, attended the school where his father worked. Frank was an active member of the Long Ditton Church Lads Brigade and used to work for a local baker as a delivery boy, taking the bread around the village by cart to people's homes. His brother, Jack, was also a pupil at the school and went on to join the Royal Marines before becoming a representative for a seed company. He also became president of Kingston Chamber of Commerce and had a stall selling

Agnes Dymond.

plants at the Apple Market in Kingston.

Both Jack and Frank were raised at 6 South Bank, a stone's throw from Winters Bridge.

William died at the age of 70 in the bitter February month of 1947. Agnes passed away in the 1960s and during her life had been married twice. Her marriage to Alfred Bicker, who died in the First World War, had produced two daughters, Gwendoline, and Joan, who later worked for Dr Barnardo's.

In 1998, Joan lived in retirement at Durrington, near Worthing. After leaving South Bank, Gwendoline married and lived in Chessington, then at 296 Hook Road, Hook, until her death in 1996. She had one son, David Tippett Wilson, who took on the Hook Road house after his mother's death.

Long Ditton School, the Rushett. It opened in 1873 and served the village for 100 years.

Jack Dymond: Ditton boy who joined Royal Marines.

Frank Dymond: baker's boy in the Church Lads Brigade.

Joan was one of Agnes's four children who lived at South Bank.

The girls of 1905 at Long Ditton School, Rushett Road.

SURREY EDUCATION COMMITTEE
This is to Certify

That *Alec Coxhead*

Attending *Long Ditton Mixed* School

MADE·FULL·ATTENDANCE·FOR·THE·TERM

Ending *Midsummer 1906*

Chairman of Managers C.R.W. Hughes

Head Teacher

Alec Coxhead's good attendance certificate in midsummer 1906.

Some of the children at Long Ditton School in about 1908.

Strokes of cane for idleness, laziness, but they laughed it off

Old-fashioned discipline in school

CORPORAL punishment was a normal way of life in most Surrey schools in the first half of the 20th century. And Long Ditton was no exception. Two or three strokes of the cane were frequently given if children were naughty.

A glance at the old log books recalls some memorable moments for pupils. Strokes were given by Welsh schoolmaster J E Roberts in September 1927 to five pupils for "inattention during drawing lesson," while Mr E Quick administered the same punishment just days apart for "laziness in drill" and "idleness, lying and stealing".

Mrs L Brain resorted to the cane when other children were found to be "playing with a ruler" and showing "untidiness".

Mrs Brain also recorded incidents of "cheat-ing, carelessness and disobedience."

In February 1930, Mr Roberts used the stick on eight pupils for "careless and dirty work" while in January 1931, a nine-year-old child was punished for "throwing a peel".

Putting paint on a boy's face, cycling in the playground, creating a disturbance, splashing ink and talking in science, were deemed punishable with a stroke of the cane in the early 1930s. Although it was mostly boys who were caned, some girls were treated likewise.

Children used to recite a poem about Mr Quick:

Mr Quick don't forget to give you the stick
When he does, he makes you dance
Out of England into France
Out of France and into Spain
Over the hill and back again.

First day at Long Ditton

SYBIL Tranter was a bright young girl and while at Tiffin Girls' School, Kingston, she decided to make teaching her career.

After training to be a teacher at Brighton, she returned to Surrey and in the early 1930s was accepted for a post at St Matthew's Senior Girls School in Surbiton – just a mile from Long Ditton.

Around this time, her family decided that their house in Kingston was no longer suitable for their needs and they moved to Branton, a spacious house in Portsmouth Avenue, Thames Ditton.

Miss Tranter had four sisters: Elsie, Janet, Winifred, and Esme. Although Elsie and Esme married, the other three remained single and shared a life together, living in the same homes for all of their lives.

Although she says she was happy at St Matthew's, Sybil had a yearning to run her own school and was delighted when accepted for the post of headmistress at Long Ditton Church of England School at Rushett Road in February 1941.

Her joy soon faded, however, when she realised she had joined a run-down school with hardly any staff and one female teacher who told her: "I've never worked for a woman and I don't intend to now!"

Many of the problems she faced stemmed from the fact the war had already started and that a new school for senior pupils had just opened at Hinchley Wood in 1940. Most the staff had transferred there and had taken with them much of the school equipment. Most the men had been called up for war service.

Miss Tranter, who recalled that 15 of her ancestors and mothers were teachers, wrote in her memoirs: "When I arrived on my first day, I found very inadequate staff. One class of 40 were without a teacher and the seven-year-olds were being kept in the infants department until a teacher could be found for them." She continues the story:

"New staff were to be appointed in September when new young teachers were leaving college. I thought I could manage quite well until September until I was horrified to find some cupboards without the necessary text books. I was told that some books had gone to the senior school when the seniors left, and all the money used for buying school equipment had been taken by the Government for guns, ammunition, aeroplanes and the like.

Some of the girls at Long Ditton School, Rushett Road, in 1919. In that year, Miss Tranter was aged 11 and about to become a pupil at Tiffin Girls' School in Kingston.

Even part of the teachers' salaries had been taken, but was returned after the war.

I was desperate for the necessary text books, but I was told that at the County Hall, Kingston, there were many books available that had been returned from schools as 'not wanted'.

At the end of my first day, I cycled to the County Hall after school and I was taken to the basement where there were piles of text books all over the floor in dusty heaps. It may have been dust to them, but to me it was gold dust.

I quickly went through the piles and made a list of all I could use and arranged to have them sent to the school.

Now I felt school life could become more or less normal when the new teachers arrived in September. But we still had the very old building, and as the days became colder,

The first car Miss Tranter's family owned — a 1928 Singer which they gave the pet name Philomel.

we had to start our own fires.

We had open fires or coal fires in each room. The caretaker came at six o'clock each morning and had the fires blazing away by the time the children came and the rooms were reasonably warm.

However, as the days got colder, they got shorter, and the nights longer. Then the caretaker had a visit from the air raid wardens. They told him he was breaking the black-out regulations. No fire must be lit before eight o'clock, and all must be raked out by 2.30pm.

Our rooms became bitterly cold, and I wrote in the log book on several occasions ' . . .no room has reached 40 degrees (F) all day'.

Today, a school without adequate heating would be closed. But this was war-time. Most of their mothers were engaged in war work, and in any case, the children would be going home to a war-time dinner, and sleeping at the bottom of the garden in an Anderson shelter, with only a hot water bottle for warmth, so no one complained.

It was at this time that the Government realised the children were not getting enough to eat, so we started hot school dinners. But, of course, we had no kitchen and no dining room. Very few schools had. So we had to eat the meals in the classrooms.

A kitchen was needed for keeping meals hot and washing up. The council used a little dingy, unused cloakroom in the school for this. A deep sink was put in place of the little wash basins, a very old, second-hand gas stove was fixed for keeping meals hot, and a very old water heater indeed was installed. That water heater had seen better days and deeply resented our dingy little kitchen.

The dinners were to be cooked in a central kitchen and brought to the schools each day by voluntary helpers, who would be given petrol coupons for this service. Our helpers were all kindly folk, but some were older, and carrying the metal containers into school was quite hard work, so we allowed some of the older boys to help. This usually worked well, but on one occasion, I heard a shout. One of the lids had come off on a gravy container. I hurried out to the car and found my lady helper sitting with a foot on the brake and the other on the clutch, while the gravy ran round the floor.

We cleared up the car as well as we could, but that helper would not be coming again.

We had voluntary helpers in the kitchen, serving the dinners and washing up afterwards. But that water heater was a real trial. It would wait until I had got my most valued helper and it would start to growl and shake a little. Then, without warn-

ing, it would make a large bang, and blow boiling steam out into the kitchen and my helper would run away screaming.

This kindly helper, too, would not be coming again. Although the heater was repaired, it always happened again and new ones could not be bought in war-time.

After this happened several times, I found I had no helpers. There were 200 dirty plates on the draining boards and no-one to wash them. All the teachers were busy with their classes. The plates were needed the next day. So you can guess who had to wash them.

I told the education committee I could not accept dinners with that boiler. But no other boiler could be found, so they said they would give me a paid helper who would have to give a week's notice.

We found a very good helper and I warned her to get outside quickly at the first growl from the boiler and we could then manage. But that was not the end of our dinner troubles. Because we had no dining hall, the children had to eat at their desks. These were dual desks with sloping tops. That was all right for the older ones, but a seven-year-old with a fork in one hand and a knife in the other could not stop the plate slipping down the desk and the child would be crying with a hot dinner in her lap. Again, I complained to the education authorities and we were given trestle tables and forms to put up each day in front of the class.

Now, life was becoming more orderly and schooldays were passing quite happily. The children worked hard and sat for their common entrance exams as before, in those very cold classrooms. If the teacher saw that their hands were too cold to write, she would say: 'Jump about and clap your hands!' and the children would go jumping round the room and laughing until they were warm and ready to start work again.

We had our usual Nativity play at Christmas. Of course, we could not get all the necessary costumes, but the Wise Men looked quite smart in dressing gowns.

Of course, we had the usual air raids occasionally, but that didn't seem to worry the children. At the first sound of the siren, they picked up their gas masks and ran across the playground to the air raid shelters.

The shelters were narrow and dark with no chance of reading or writing. So, as soon as they got there, they started to chant their tables. 'Once two is two', right up to '12 x 12 is 144'. Then they would start at the end and go back to the beginning. There was not a child in the school that did not know their tables, which is more than could be said about our children today.

If they heard planes, and gunfire, all the war-time songs of the

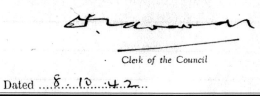

Miss Tranter was enrolled for fire-fighting duties in the Dittons area during the war. She was also given emergency feeding duties if the need arose.

day — Run Rabbit Run, and another favourite of the day, Mares Eat Oats And Does Eat Oats — would be sung. With the all-clear, they would hurry back to the classrooms.

By now, many of our children had been evacuated and I had an empty classroom. It was getting near the end of the war and everyone was talking about invasion. Our troops had cross the Channel again. If we had been invaded, all food supplies would have been cut off, so emergency food centres were started. One was to be in an empty classroom."

Lessons in bomb shelters

HEADMISTRESS Sybil Tranter was at the helm of Long Ditton Junior School at the height of the war years. Here, she recalls the tense days when invasion seemed imminent.

Emergency food centres were started in the district and one of the depots was in one of Miss Tranter's empty classrooms.

"Vans arrived with huge wooden boxes marked 'corner beef' and such like. A cooking stove was fixed up in the playground and a water tank put outside in the road and camouflaged.

I was told I had to be ready to open up the centre at any time, night or day.

Thankfully, it was never used apart from one trial run when I had to be at school at midnight.

The war was now nearly at an end when we had the most frightening thing of all — the flying bomb or doodlebug.

One morning when I went to school, I found the floor and desks in one room covered by broken glass (*after a nearby blast)* and I thought of the possibility of the children having been there. So, after that we only used the playground and shelters. They were long, weary days.

The children played while the teachers stood and listened, listened, and listened yet again for the sound of a doodlebug. If one was heard, the children would hurry into the shelters.

But one day — 20th June 1944 — our story nearly ended. We heard a doodlebug much louder than usual, and coming straight towards us. We quickly got the children into the shelters. They couldn't sing now. We told them to lie on the floor and cover their faces with their hands.

We could hear the 'imminent danger' ringing at the next door garage where they were doing war work. We hoped and hoped the bomb would pass over, but the engine stopped and we knew it was falling.

I suppose it was a matter of seconds before the explosion, but to us waiting, it seemed to be hours. After the explosion, we told the children to sit up again, and those children were really marvellous. Not one even said 'Oh!'.

I walked down through the shelter to see if they were all right. I noticed one little girl's knee was shaking. I touched it as I passed, and said 'Are you all right?'. She smiled at me and said 'Oh yes. I'm sorry. I was just resting on a nerve'. Now that was a nine-year-old girl, who knew quite well that she had been within yards of death. No wonder I thought my children were wonderful.

Mothers gather at Long Ditton recreation ground to see their children taking part in the school sports day on 27th June 1951. On the right is the rector, Rev John Harvey.

I opened the shelter door to see if the school was still standing but the bomb had fallen (*in Thorkhill Road)* on houses across the road near the school, and one was completely destroyed and others damaged. Friends we had known we would not see again.

The recreation ground opposite was covered with white, like a snowstorm — the remains of what a few minutes before had been homes. Lace curtains hung from the trees.

We could not let the children out into the confusion of the street outside, so we kept them there until someone came to fetch them. They were all covered in a fine yellow powder.

Soon after the war ended — and with the summer holidays upon us — we felt we could have a rest. I had been down to five pupils.

When war was eventually over, all we wanted to do was rest. On the first night of peace, I went to my bedroom (*at home in Portsmouth Avenue)* to sleep in my bed — the first time for some years. I pulled back the curtains with no fear of the blackout and a heavy thunderstorm which was raging.

I looked at the bright flashes of the lightning and listened to the crash of the thunder and I felt how much more wonderful were the works of nature than the explosions of guns and bombs of mankind."

With the war behind her, Miss Tranter had to think about planning a new school but the idea was shelved while existing problems were tackled. Bomb damage had to be repaired and new toilets built. The toilets were replaced in a new shed which was fitted with hot and cold water.

The school had to wait its turn to have its bomb damage repaired but great anxiety was caused by broken plaster in the ceiling of one of the classrooms. Miss Tranter feared that vibrations from trains nearby, or lorries, could bring debris crashing down onto the pupils.

"I 'phoned the education officer once again and asked if he would take responsibility if a child was injured. The ceiling was repaired next day."

With so many men folk still abroad, waiting for a discharge from the army, builders and workmen at home were scarce.

In the following decade, Miss Tranter and her staff made a concerted effort to find a site for a new school. They thought they had found one — just off Angel Road — but their attempts were thwarted by red tape. The site was in *Thames* Ditton.

A wedding in dimly-lit St Mary's Church, Long Ditton, took place despite the church windows being boarded up after damage from a doodlebug in 1944.

Doodlebugs wreak havoc in Long Ditton

DURING the summer of 1944, Hitler aimed his most deadly weapon at Britain — the V1 flying bombs, or doodlebugs as they were known.

Two of the pilotless flying bombs detonated in Long Ditton. One exploded next to St Mary's Church, causing extensive damage in the vicinity of Green Hedges and the church. The other destroyed two houses in Thorkhill Road and almost demolished the lower parish hall on the corner of Ewell Road. Two women and a girl aged 13 were later reported killed in the Thorkhill Road blast, although a news blackout on the effects of enemy action meant that contemporary reports were deliberately vague.

The explosion at Thorkhill Road occurred after a flying bomb, said to have been seen from Winters Bridge travelling in the direction of Hampton Court, suddenly changed direction in a gust of wind.

A Ferry Road resident, Patrick Bennett, later wrote: "The motor cut out over the Mason's Arms and the bomb landed along Thorkhill Road. Some young children near the river side *(of Portsmouth Road)* on what is now City Wharf, had a grandstand view of this spectacular event."

Alan Rackley, born at 32 Fleece Road in 1927, was 16 years old at the time of the Thorkhill Road bomb. He was cycling along Ewell Road near Long Ditton Junior School when the explosion occurred.

His memory of that moment stayed with him for the rest of his life.

A pair of houses in Victoria Avenue, Surbiton, next to the Balaclava Road recreation ground, were destroyed by a flying bomb.

"I heard it coming, but took no notice. I looked up again and thought: 'Bloomin' heck, it's coming straight towards me'. It just kept coming nearer. I jumped off my bike and buried my head in the gutter. The vibration was so great, you felt like the road was coming up and hitting you in the face. It was all over in a flash.

"I then went straight down the road towards the hall. There was dust and smoke everywhere. A poor United Dairies horse belonging to the milkman was lying in the road covered in bricks, rubble and wood. I think the horse got up in the end but I don't think it survived.

"The milk cart was outside the houses that caught the blast. It was horrific but I did not take too much notice; there was so much going on at the time. It was just one of those incidents. There was nothing you could do. If anyone was in the house, they would have been killed. I understand a mother and her daughter were killed."

Mr Rackley recalled that the 1907 parish hall "was blown apart," and children were upset that the tin hall behind was razed.

Church, houses and hall wrecked
War at Balaclava

LONG Ditton's lower parish hall, in Ewell Road, was badly damaged by the doodlebug in 1944.

At the time it was being used as a British Restaurant to offer affordable meals to local families. This service was permanently halted by the flying bomb.

Witnesses recall the doodlebug diving through gardens before exploding and causing considerable damage at the corner of Thorkhill Road and Ewell Road.

Headmistress Sybil Tranter's experiences at the school in nearby Rushett Road have been described in an earlier chapter but it seems relevant at this point to recall her poignant memory of seeing lace curtains draped from the trees on the recreation ground after the explosion.

Others recall a flurry of papers falling from the

Surbiton Baptist Church before being demolished by a flying bomb in Balaclava Road.

St Andrew's Hall in Balaclava Road was demolished along with the Surbiton Baptist Church next door when a doodlebug struck on 21st August 1944. Both were rebuilt.

sky. It is said they originated from a clinic operating at the hall. The documents carpeted the recreation field.

Throughout the war period, the rector of Long Ditton was Rev Robert Wilson. He had held the post since 1921 and was to stay until 1946.

Many remembered him for his sense of humour, his bike which he more often took for a walk than rode, his learned sermons and devotion to pastoral duties.

The summer of 1944 must have been a gruelling time for him, especially after fatalities

were reported after the Thorkhill Road incident.

The other doodlebug came down next to St Mary's Church, close to neighbouring house, Green Hedges.

Witness Alan Rackley, the 16-year-old employee of the London and Home Counties Joint Electricity Board, later recalled:"The damage to the church was terrible. GIs turned up in General Motor Company lorries but there was nothing they could do."

All the windows in the north and south walls were blown out except for the Queen Victoria

diamond jubilee glasswork which was damaged but able to be repaired.

Much of the metalwork of the windows was contorted and shards of glass were strewn everywhere. The windows remained boarded up from June 1944 to 1950.

In Balaclava Road, Surbiton Baptist Church, built 1905, was demolished, but replaced in November 1955. Next door's St Andrew's Hall was razed and later rebuilt. The Baptists originally worshipped in 1898 in a wooden hall opposite, which had been used by the Chelsea Water Company's men for social meetings.

Ditton's post-war years remembered
Plans for a new school

YEARS of planning and frustration had to be endured in the post-war years before headmistress Miss Sybil Tranter and her staff eventually saw their dream of a new, larger St Mary's School come to fruition.

Some 30 years of difficulties were suffered at the old school in Rushett Road which saw an increasing number of pupils squeezed in for lessons.

The school came under the Diocese of Southwark and in suburbs closer than Long Ditton to London, there was much devastation to be attended to. Miss Tranter had to be patient for a long time. The problem of overcrowding was made worse for children were returning from evacuation more quickly than she had predicted.

Some years later, a parent teacher association (PTA) was formed and mothers and fathers willingly gave their time and efforts to help the school with its problems.

Lunch-hour difficulties were largely overcome when the Parish Hall was eventually rebuilt after the war damage it experienced. It was able to be used as a dining hall and for other school activities. The recreation ground at Ewell Road was used for games and sports.

A site was then earmarked for a new school. It was in Angel Road. Joy turned to sorrow when it was found that the site was just into Thames Ditton and fell under the Diocese of Guildford, and could not proceed because of this. Finding another plot in Long Ditton was not easy.

However, some time later, Barr's nurseries on the corner of Sugden Road and Ewell Road went up for sale. The nurseries had given this corner of the village a big splash of colour for many decades.

The land was purchased and the plot used for building a new school. In the first phase of construction a modern kitchen and hall were built where, at last, meals could be cooked on site and eaten. The dining hall had a sliding glass partition enabling it to be converted into two classrooms when the need arose. There was also a cloakroom and a small room used as a staff dining area.

The happiness of having this new hall was rather short-lived. It was found that many dangers faced the boys and girls as they daily walked between the school in Rushett Road and the new hall in Sugden Road.

The main hazard was the bridge in Ewell Road. It had no guard

Deputy headmistress Mrs E V Winfield and teacher Mr Hudson with pupils at a show in the 1950s.

rail and the pavement under the arch was only 18 inches wide.

Miss Tranter recalled: " A teacher had to stand in the road each lunchtime to see the children did not step off the pavement for the noise of passing trains deadened the sound of approaching traffic.

In addition, the bridge had been damaged in the war. Each time a train passed, gravel fell from the arch, forcing the children to scatter.

Said Miss Tranter: "I asked British Rail to repair the bridge but I was told they had hundreds of bridges to repair and it would have to wait for the time being. One day, as the children were passing underneath, several large pieces of stone fell to the ground, narrowly missing them. I was so anxious about the safety of the children, I picked up the stones and carried them to the Education Office, saying that miraculously, the stones had not injured the children, but I could not use the bridge pathway. The bridge was then repaired, the guard rail erected and the pave-

ment widened."

Miss Tranter's battle with the authorities was backed by a vociferous rector, Rev Eric Smith, who wrote to the powers-that-be just after the canteen opened at Sugden Road on Tuesday 4th September 1973. He described the situation as a nightmare. On the first day, there was a deluge of rain and passing cars left the youngsters drenched. He reported that 128 children had to daily make this "10 minute precarious journey" at lunchtimes, and he feared a fatal accident unless there was remedial action.

And, he added, " . . . having arrived at the canteen, wet through, coats and macintoshes are put on the floor as there are not enough coat hooks, and those that are there are far too low. Then, to crown the whole muddle, they have to have a cold meal of bully beef, because the builders have hidden the gas pipe under four inches of tarmacadam." They had not finished their work and had left 'craters', which, said Mr Smith, the children had to clamber over.

Villagers celebrate Christmas at Long Ditton Parish Hall. The hall was damaged in a flying bomb attack in 1944 and was rebuilt. Among those at the re-opening ceremony was Mrs 'Willie' Stevenson of Eaglehurst, St Mary's Road, who raised funds to build the hall in 1907.

Rev John Harvey

Rev John Harvey was Rector of St Mary's Church, Long Ditton, from 1946 to 1956. He succeeded Rev Robert Wilson. He is pictured here at a garden fete in the Rectory gardens at 67 St Mary's Road, Long Ditton.

Mr Harvey had to pick up the pieces of parish life after the war and revive its activities. He oversaw the efforts in the village to rebuild the Parish Hall at Ewell Road and to repair the damage to the church after the flying bomb attack.

Rev Frederick Burt

PICTURED above is Rev Frederick Burt with the churchwardens and choir at St Mary's Church, Long Ditton, on a spring day during Mr Burt's incumbency between 1956 and 1967. Mr Burt was a single man and a seafarer connected with the Seafarers' Society. It has been said that he would never speak of his war experiences. Parishioners remember there were often "Mission For Seamen" services held at the church. He lived in the Rectory, St Mary's Road, by himself. He retired in 1967 and moved to a home in Warninglid, Sussex, where he later later died.

On the left is a display of maypole dancing at a fete in the garden of the Rectory, St Mary's Road, in 1950. Rev John Harvey can be identified in the background, on the left, watching the entertainment.

Some Long Ditton crimes — and tragedies

SATURDAY, NOV. 21, 1874.

CHARGE OF WIFE MURDER.

Late last night a man named George Poplet, a labourer, was brought to the police station charged with murdering a woman supposed to be his wife. From what we could ascertain at midnight, it seems that P.S. Davey, of Thames Ditton, received information which led him to go to Waffron's Farm, Thames Ditton, where he found a woman lying dead, death having resulted, by the doctor's statement, from the effects of a stab in the body. It was believed that the man who had been seen with the deceased had made his way towards Ewell. Sergeant Davey and P.C. Seares at once followed, and from the description given them they took a man into custody at Ewell last night just before 10, and lodged him safely in Kingston station, whence he will be taken this morning before the County justices.

Latest news from the Surrey Comet of 21st November 1874.

POLICE at Winters Bridge hurried to Waffrons Farm, Woodstock Lane, on Friday 20th November 1874, after a report of a woman stabbed to death.

Some time later, George Poplet was arrested at Ewell and at Kingston was charged with murdering his wife, Charlotte, at the farm with a knife. A farm labourer had heard screams and investigated. The *Surrey Comet* reported: "Poplet showed no remorse at all, saying she had left him and their three little children for another man. He had no regrets whatsoever. If she didn't live with him, he would not see her working nearby with a threshing machine.

"His lordship, having put on the black cap, proceeded to pass sentence of death. Sentence of death was then passed in the usual form and prisoner was removed from the dock still unmoved. Thus, in the space of seven days, the awful crime was committed, brought home to the murderer and sentence of death passed upon him."

CHILD MURDER BY A STEP-MOTHER

Before the Kingston-on-Thames county magistrates, Ellen Shepherd, aged 35, residing at the Rushett, Long Ditton, has been charged with the wilful murder of her step-son, John Griffiths, eight months old, by drowning him in a water butt. From the evidence it appears that on returning home from school on a given afternoon, prisoner told her step-daughter, aged eight years, that she would never see Johnnie again, and directly afterwards, the child saw the baby in the water-butt close to the back door. She at once fetched her father, who was working close by, but upon his arrival, he found the child dead. He asked his wife what she had been doing, when she replied, "I know what I have done; I have put him in the water butt." Having communicated with a neighbour, who took the child from the butt, the husband went for the police. In reply to the magistrates, this witness stated that hitherto his wife had always been kind to the child, but for the previous few days had been drinking, and upon telling her of this she threatened to drown the child like a cat in the water-butt.

When taken into custody by Police-sergeant Brooks, prisoner said, "I did it; I told him (her husband) I would do it last night." She then seemed to be recovering from the effects of drink, and appeared to be stupefied. At the station, the sergeant, in reply, to Inspector Rushbridge, mentioned that the doctor told him the child had been in the water three or four hours, whereupon prisoner instantly remarked, "that cannot be; for I did not put him in until three o'clock." Prisoner, who had nothing to say, and refrained from asking any questions, was committed for trial at the assizes.

This child killing inquiry at The Rushett, was reported in the Epsom Herald on Saturday 19th July 1884.

INQUESTS.

DOUBLE TRAGEDY AT LONG DITTON.

A double tragedy, revealed by the discovery last Wednesday of the dead bodies of Ethel Maggie White, 28, wife of Geo. Fredk. White, coal porter, of Rectory-lane, Long Ditton, and her child Mabel, aged six months,

Ethel White, 28, and her baby went missing from their Rectory Lane home on Christmas Eve c1910 and were found drowned in the river at Claremont Wharf by a punter. She had been depressed.

A sign at the top of Ditton Hill c1907, put up by the Cyclists' Touring Club reads: "Cyclists, ride with caution." Sadly, this did not prevent a vicar being killed by a cyclist in 1917.

Vicar killed at Ditton Hill

IN THE autumn of 1917, the vicar of Tavistock, Devonshire, for 22 years, met with his death "under peculiarly sad circumstances" on Ditton Hill..

The *Surrey Comet* reported that the "reverend gentleman, H Godfray Le Noveu, had come to Surbiton for a few days' holiday and was staying in Langley Avenue with relatives. He was walking down Ditton Hill on a Thursday afternoon when a cyclist from Tolworth, who was riding on the proper side of the road behind Rev Le Noveu, drew out to the right in order, it is said, to avoid a dog. Simultaneously, he rang his bell and the clergyman, who was a few yards ahead, stepped sharply to the right. As a result he was struck by the bicycle and thrown heavily to the ground." The report continued: "He sustained severe injuries to the head and when picked up it was found that he was dead." The body was taken to Surbiton police station and then to Ditton Mortuary.

Sad fate of headmaster and wife

ONE of the most tragic incidents in Long Ditton's history occurred in July 1918 when James Mileham, the headmaster of the C of E Schools at Rushett Road for 14 years, suffered a nervous breakdown and hanged himself in the schoolhouse scullery. Two days later, his wife was found hanging in the lavatory of the same house. They are buried at Long Ditton.

Charles H Clayton, his family and Church Lads Brigade

Charles S Clayton and "his" Long Ditton Church Lads Brigade in about 1910.

Charles Hoghton Clayton and Lydia Clayton of Hillside, St Mary's Road. He lived to the age of 101.

Charles S Clayton gives a Sunday School treat at The Elms, Ditton Hill Road, in 1922. Mr Clayton died in 1951.

THE name Clayton is synonymous with Long Ditton and Ditton Hill. For many decades, the Clayton family worked tirelessly for young people in the village and were great benefactors to the community as a whole. Charles Stephen, son of Charles Hoghton Clayton, for many decades ran the Church Lads Brigade.

The family name has been immortalised in Clayton Road which links Woodstock Lane in the parish of Long Ditton to Hook where the Claytons first set up home. The family home of John and Emily Clayton was at Haycroft, Hook, (long since replaced by the Ace Parade shops). Their son, Charles Hoghton, born 1836, became a prominent London solicitor like his father. He married solicitor's daughter, Lydia Hare, of Gosbury Hall, Hook, in June 1868.

The couple set up home at Hillside, St Mary's Road, Long Ditton — on Cockcrow Hill — in 1882 and there they remained for the rest of their lives.

Charles H Clayton lived to the ripe old age of 101 and even at 100, was still managing to take a walk around the village twice a day.

On the occasion of his 100th birthday, 600 villagers and friends signed a special book for him. It was inscribed by "everyone from Bishop Hill to the taxi-men and postmen," As it was the day after the death of King George's death, it was feared that no telegram would be received. However, one arrived — from King Edward VIII — probably the first of its kind.

Some time later, he fell and broke his arm. It upset his balance and he could no longer take his daily constitutionals. He died on 17th March 1937. In July that year, his wife passed away aged 92.

Charles S Clayton.

Major Charles S Clayton

Swimming lessons in the Elms pool

CHARLES H Clayton and his wife, Lydia, had 11 children, one of whom was Charles Stephen Clayton. Major Charles S Clayton was well known to hundreds of young men and boys in Long Ditton.

Born in 1871, he had moved to The Elms, off Ditton Hill Road, by 1915, and remained there until at least 1948.

The Elms, which dated back to before the 1850s, had large wooded gardens, lawns and a swimming pool which children used to have lessons in. The property had earlier been called Elm Cottage. The grounds would once have stretched downhill towards the area where the Fleece Road shops were built in 1905. Parts of the gardens were sold off in the mid 1950s for housing and the large house was pulled down about 1960. A smaller house, no 50 still carries the name in modern times.

Later more houses were built in the grounds and these became 48 and 48a Ditton Hill Road. This road was altered to run through part of the grounds and a lay-by outside the infants school was formed from part of the original road.

Pat Rainbow, a villager for all of her life, once recalled how Mr C S Clayton, a single man, was most strict about who was admitted to the pool in his grounds.

"A lot of us used to go round to the Elms when we were children at school. If the girls went round on a Tuesday, he used to take us for swimming and teach us to swim and a Mrs Betts (*remembered in Betts Way*) used to teach us to swim, too.

"The only reason he would allow us in on a Tuesday is if we went to church on Sundays. If we did not go to church on Sundays, he would not let us in."

The joyous sounds of the children splashing around in the pool, using tyres, could be heard by people using the ancient alleyway which leads from Ditton Hill Road to Rectory Lane.

This passage was known as Hart's alley after the police officers by that name who lived for many years next door at 2 Chestnut Villas (54 Ditton Hill Road) from 1954. Sgt H Hart lived there from 1893 to 1894 and then Henry Hart was chief householder from 1895 to 1936. Thereafter, Miss E Hart lived there until the mid1950s.

It was the Church Lads Brigade C S Clayton will be remembered for. For many years he was the officer commanding a thriving Church Lads Brigade in the village which met at the Parish Hall, Ewell Road.

After his death in 1951, the brigade "soon seemed to fade away" although many other youth groups later sprang up.

A couple at work in the Rectory Lane allotments prior to the building of Betts Way. Allotments stretched along Ewell Road to the railway bridge, next to which was an orchard.

Barr's Nurseries — and the magnificent tulips

THOUSANDS of rail passengers in the 1920s knew Long Ditton not by its name but by the beauty which beheld them when passing on the train. A magnificent splash of colour took their breath away as they hurtled past Barr's nurseries which covered several acres of land at Sugden Road where the new school was built in 1974.

Writer Eric Parker made these comments in 1923. He added: "You are looking at the best of Long Ditton when you see Barr's nursery gardens from the train window. There is hardly a month in the year, except in the deep mid-winter, when the Ditton Hill gardens are not full of blossom. Railways have the good luck to run by many nursery gardens; the tulips at Ditton Hill would help the South Western to challenge any line."

The *Surrey Comet* in 1908 also had nothing but praise for the tulips.

"Lovers of beauty in the floral world will be amply repaid should they choose to visit the nurseries of Messrs Barr and Sons, of Long Ditton, where, for a space of about three acres, it is possible to wander amongst flowers displaying a wealth of most beautiful colour.

"The reputation which Messrs Barr and Sons have for the cultivation of that favourite spring flower, the daffodil, is equally maintained in the hybridizing of the tulip, a bulb which originally came to this country from Constantinople. In a visit paid to the nurseries on Monday afternoon, a representative of the *Surrey Comet* was shown around the tulip beds and was struck by the remarkable success that had been achieved in producing such a magnificent blending of shade in many varieties."

Ewell Road, Long Ditton, soon after the houses were built in about 1930.

A creeper-covered Pound Farm, replaced in the 1930s by Pound Close. Early maps show a pound for stray animals in Fleece Road next to the farm.

Victorian Ewell Road before the development of Effingham Road.

Ape, monkey, and Adolph at the Manor

THE magnificent Manor House in Woodstock Lane was once the home of lords of the manor but in more modern times has been the residence of the chairman of A C Cars, Derek Hurlock, and recently, a Japanese religious order.

George Evelyn, grandfather of the diarist John Evelyn, purchased the manor of Long Ditton in 1567 and built himself the original Manor House next to the church. Later generations of the family may have extended or rebuilt the house. Sir Peter King came to the Manor in the early 1700s and became Lord Chancellor of England on 1st June 1725. Successive generations of the King family later occupied the grand old mansion. Clayton Road, off Woodstock Lane, in the parish of Long Ditton, used to be known as Lord King's Lane as late as 1898. In 1901, two well-known parishioners living at the Manor House, Mr and Mrs Trollope, died within 10 days of each other. A church lych-gate was erected in their memory.

A German couple, the Von Ernsthausens, occupied the house at the time of the first world war and managed to remain popular with most villagers throughout the conflict, but they changed their name to Howeson. One of the sons was called Adolph. The family kept an ape, monkey and parrots during their residence. Mr Adolph Von Ernsthausen changed his name to Mr Howeson. Later, George Blay, whose firm pulled down the Rectory for redevelopment just after his death, moved in but died about 1936. In 1948, William Hurlock bought the house. He first viewed it in dense fog and took an instant liking to it. Prototypes of the hovercraft were reportedly tested on its lake.

Three views of the Manor House and grounds in 1958 prior to refurbishment.

Effingham Road in the early 1930s, looking towards Surbiton. In the 1970s, Elton John's record producer Gus Dudgeon lived at no 50. He was responsible for perfecting songs such as Goodbye Yellow Brick Road.

Builders at work on homes in Kings Road.

Building of Kings Road, 1904

KINGS Road was built in 1904 on part of Curnick's paddocks surrounding the former Upper Ditton House. A grocer's shop, also open on Sundays for items missed off the family roast shopping list, traded for years in one of the cottages. Villagers recall ice cream made from frozen custard being for sale. For a time the shop was known as Farley's. Village athlete Harold Old lived at Sunny Brae. Dennis Perrin, at Stowe Villa, was a leading cyclist in the south and won many trophies for 25, 50 and 100-mile races. In the 1940s, he rode for the Clarence Wheelers. Stokes the builders were residents of Kings Road for decades.

The opening of the Lambeth Water Company works at Long Ditton in 1852. Below, the filter beds in the 1930s. Long Ditton recreation ground, bottom left, is still allotments.

The waterworks

THERE was jubilation in Long Ditton in 1852 when the Lambeth Water Company works opened at Seething Wells. Before then, there had been only wells, pumps and dirty, open tanks.

When the Lambeth works at Portsmouth Road opened after four years of building works, residents were overjoyed that at last a bright, modern way of getting clean tap water had been established in the district. The *Surrey Comet* commented: "On taking a view of these monuments of mechanical skill and manual labour, one cannot but be filled with astonishment and inhale an inspiration of grateful emotion."

A special train was laid on to bring 250 visitors from Waterloo. The band of the Coldstream Guards entertained and directors splashed out £1 per head on a lavish buffet. In 1998 the redundant water works re-opened as a £6million health and leisure centre, The Pinnacle Club, retaining much of the old architecture

The works were the design of brilliant architect James Simpson who also designed Southend Pier among other structures.

The Ditton works in the 1850s comprised an intake from the river, sand filter beds, a boiler plant and four compound beam engines pumping to a reservoir at Brixton.

Many of the staff at the plant lived in terraced cottages in Howard Street, Prospect Place, Winters Road, Claremont Terrace and South Bank.

The Chelsea Waterworks Company then opened a works in 1856 on an adjacent site just across the Ditton boundary in Seething Wells. The two companies were absorbed into the Metropolitan Water Board at its creation in 1902.

Further river pollution necessitated the construction of a new intake and reservoir at Molesey in 1903; the water being transferred by brick culvert to Ditton for filtration and pumping. The Lambeth and Chelsea works were re-modelled between 1930 and 1932, the old steam engine plant being replaced by steam turbines driving centrifugal pumps.

The water board built homes for staff in Akerman Road and Seething Wells Lane, just over the border in Surbiton, later in the 20th century. The area has always been a favourite haunt of midges in summer. Columns of the insects waver above trees and the micro thermals above people's heads in Balaclava Road area.

In the mid 1990s, controversy was sparked by plans to build extensive flats and a housing estate on the waterworks site in addition to the student accommodation sanctioned for part of the site.

Sgt Blake probes 'murder'
Police station

Police Station, Ferry Road.

DITTONS police station in Ferry Road served a large area, including Molesey. After the 1930s, officers moved out and the old police house was turned into a private dwelling which was still standing in 1998.

One of its most colourful characters was Sgt Ernest Blake who spent more years in retirement than in his police career. One night he rode off on his bicycle to probe a reported murder. A bloodied man had been found lying at Manor Farm, Woodstock Lane. The inquiry was scaled down when it was found he had been kicked by a horse.

PC Amos.

Sgt Blake, who lived at 37 Ditton Hill Road, lived to a great age. When finally he was so frail he went into hospital, not expecting to return, his wife gave a neighbour her husband's bottle of Scotch. Sgt Blake recovered, was sent home, and went hunting for the Scotch.

Another officer, PC Maitland Amos, a "placid man", was "good at dealing with scrumping".

Filling up for petrol on 14th October 1955 at Comerford's premises on the river side of Portsmouth Road.

Remarkable religious find by widowed twins
Swaynesthorpe adventurers

LONG before the modern houses in today's Devonshire Drive were built, there stood a large house called Swaynesthorpe, set in four acres of grounds.

In the 1880s, Swaynesthorpe became home to twin sisters. Their love of travel and foreign languages would lead to one of the most famous discoveries of the Biblical world.

Margaret and Agnes Smith were born in the 1840s. They were brought up in Ayrshire, Scotland, and it became clear that they had an incredible talent for foreign languages. Indeed, by their mid-twenties, they were proficient in Hebrew and Arabic.

When their father died, the twins boldly set about their first major expedition through the Holy Land and Egypt. A description of their adventure was published in 1870 in a book called Eastern Pilgrims.

Margaret first settled at Ditton Hill in 1883, when she married James Gibson, a celebrated translator. Soon afterwards, Agnes also came to live at the house. However, tragedy struck in 1886 with the death of Margaret's husband. A year later, Agnes married Samuel Lewis, a Cambridge University librarian, at St Mary's, Long Ditton. Four years later, her husband also died. To offset their grief, the twins went travelling extensively. In 1891, they joined forces with a Cambridge friend Rendel Harris who had earlier visited Egypt and the Convent of St Catherine on Mount Sinai. There, he had found a version of a lost Christian document. He fired the twins' imagination and convinced them more discoveries awaited them. The sisters left Cairo on 30th January 1892 and, after an arduous nine-day trek, arrived at the convent on 7th February. The intrepid travellers became friendly with the prior, who gave them special access to several manuscripts. Among these was a group of documents dating back to 778AD. But the sisters noticed that an even earlier text was partially visible underneath. Later analysis revealed this earlier text to be the oldest surviving copy of the four Gospels. The Long Ditton twins' remarkable findings were published two years later — in 1894 — a true reflection of the ladies' extraordinary learning and sense of adventure.

Comerford's showrooms, Portsmouth Road, on a February day in 1952. The prices of the cars in front range from £118 to £345.

Part of the forecourt of Root's Motors (left); Hungerford Villas (centre) and Comerford's show-rooms, Portsmouth Road, in about 1965.

Schoolboy cousins Ron Smith and Fred Rainbow (right) at the front gate of 6 Rectory Lane in the late 1920s. Fred was still living at the same house in 1998.

Morris Minors for £366

IN this picture, taken in about 1965, the forecourt of Root's Motors is displaying a number of fashionable cars for sale. The 1963 Morris Minor is going for £366 and the 1964 model is on offer for £389. Next to them are a 1961 Austin A40 – £315 – and a Mini, for sale at £320.

The garage, owned by Long Ditton Motors, stood next to Hungerford Villas, seen in the centre of the picture. A list of residents for Portsmouth Road, dated 1960, indicates the occupants of the villas as Terence Nash at number 1 and James Brooks at number 2. Root's stood at the junction of Portsmouth Road and Cholmley Road.

Beyond Hungerford Villas is Comerfords Ltd, motor car agents, and on the far right of the picture, the entrance to W A Skinner and Company, the timber merchants and fencing contractors at City Wharf, established in 1920.

The bygone corner shop at Howard Street in the 1960s.

Lady cyclists and a horse-drawn carriage travel along the Portsmouth Road near the waterworks before the days of motor cars. The road used to be the main turnpike highway between Kingston and Portsmouth. Tolls had to be paid at the gates.

Collapse of Winters Bridge shops

A caped policeman guards the devastated shops at Criterion Buildings, Winters Bridge, in 1908.

THE unusual sight of the collapse of newly-erected shops was witnessed at Long Ditton on a weekday morning in 1908.

The *Surrey Comet* reported that it appeared that a builder "has been constructing two shops upon a prominent site on the Portsmouth Road, at Windows' Bridge (*sic*).

"They were attached, and it seems that the drains to the two buildings were being laid simultaneously.

"During the week, the trenches were dug in proximity to and at a level below the concrete foundation. To this and the recent bad weather conditions has been attributed the sudden sinking of the foundations to the level of the trenches. In the collapse, the outer walls of the structure sank in a converging line towards the centre and two men who were at work on the spot at the time were fortunate in escaping without injury.

"The front of the shops are in such a damaged condition that they will, in all probability, have to be rebuilt. At the rear, however, the effect of the subsidence is not so pronounced and hopes are entertained that this part of the building may be strutted up and rendered secure."

Fraud over dragging bodies from river

Essex Arms

EARLS of Essex, the de Mandevilles, who were lords of the manor of "Ditune" in the 12th century, have been recalled in Mandeville Drive, off Ditton Hill, and previously in the Essex Arms, whose name changed to the Ferry Tavern in about 1986 when landlords John and Penny Callan took over.

Compared to the long-established public houses in the area, the Essex Arms (pictured above) was a more modern addition to the Dittons' drinking houses. It opened next to the Moon and South Down Dairy and Dobbs & Son, corn chandlers, and later expanded in size. By 1925 the landlord was Henry Price.

The police station in Ferry Road was opened in about 1854 and shut around 1930. It had a mortuary next door. After its closure, the premises were at first used as a telephone exchange and then turned into flats. Hammerton's and Buttery's boat yards were also in the road and at least one cottage dates back to about 1811.

Local boys helped the ferryman for pocket money. For rowing to Hampton Court and back they received 1d of the 2d fare. Many bodies were washed up at this high point of the river. For retrieving a body from the water near the Ditton bank, 2s 6d was charged to the authorities; from the opposite bank, 3s 6d. Apparently, wily retrievers would tow corpses found on the Surrey side to the Middlesex bank and back in order to claim an extra shilling.

The dead were prepared for burial at the Ferry Road mortuary and 3s 6d (18p) was charged for this duty, often carried out by a lady who lived over the road in the 1811 cottage. She was a mother of eight.

The 201 bus

Winters Bridge trolleybus turning circle with a Kingston-bound 201 approaching and another departing.

The LT 201 bus used chiefly RF vehicles on the Dittons service. Narrow streets and parked cars caused delays. Drivers were sometimes irritated at having to stop at request stops as they tried to make up lost time.

TROLLEYBUSES replaced the trams in Portsmouth Road, Long Ditton in 1931. At first the route number was 2 but in 1933, when London Transport was formed, route 2 was re-numbered the 602. For the next 29 years, the trolleybus slipped along the Portsmouth Road — with stops at the City Arms and the Three Pigeons — to Kingston 'loop' and back to Winters Bridge.

The terminus was known as The Dittons and was the least used terminal of all London trolleybus routes. At the end of each run, the bus stood on the specially-constructed turning circle at the end of St Leonard's Road whilst the driver and conductor invariably refreshed themselves in the nearby Winters Bridge Cafe.

In 1962, the Kingston area trolleybuses were withdrawn. Route 602 was replaced by the short-lived 282 motor bus route.

The fondly-remembered 201 RF bus for many years served Long Ditton, stopping in Balaclava Road and Effingham Road and 'Ditton Schools' on the Kingston to Hampton Court route. The service's last day under London Transport was 26th September 1980. The RF vehicles had been used from the hot summer of 1959 to 6th November 1976. Conductors issued tickets until 17th November 1964 when a driver-only single-decker service started.

The 201 had its humble beginnings in Middlesex. It started as the 105 between Hounslow Garage and Hounslow Central Station in June 1931 and took in Lampton. It was extended southwards to Hanworth in October 1931. It was diverted to run to Teddington in January 1932 and extended through to Thames Ditton, Surbiton and Kingston in June 1933. The northern terminus became Lampton in 1934.

On 29th September 1980, a Monday to Friday service through the Dittons was provided by Mole Valley Transport Services, route 7 (Esher-Surbiton). There were eight changes to this route in its short life, including an extension to Kingston in 1981, and to Leatherhead in the other direction, in July of the same year. Two years later, it was cut to Monday to Friday shopping hours and in July 1985 to Mondays, Thursdays and Fridays only and served stops between Hampton Court and Kingston only. On 27th March 1986, the last of these buses ran, after which the firm stopped trading. On 3rd April 1986, Epsom Coaches started a Mondays, Thursdays and Fridays shopping return trip from Hampton Court to Kingston, numbered the 201!

On 25th April 1987, this service was absorbed into London and Country's 501 and 513, funded by Surrey County Council. Further changes ensued, with involvement from London Buses, Westlink, then Tellings Golden Miller. The more modern K3 service was increased to six days a week, half-hourly, funded by the county council.

Cholmley Villas, Portsmouth Road, c1965. In the late 1950s, residents included Philip Redman, Mrs Burton, Mrs Hardcastle, Andrew Bruce, Charles Mortimer and Henry Walter Wyatt. The entrance to Cholmley Road is on the right.

Claremont Terrace, Portsmouth Road, stood between Comerford's motorcycle premises and the public house formerly called the Masons Arms. Residents in 1959 included John Brett, Mrs Gater, Mrs Payne and Mrs Groombridge.

Hampton Terrace was on the Portsmouth Road next to Winters Road. In the late 1950s, the cottages were home to Miss Barber, Thomas Terry, Mrs M Lucas, Thomas Bicker, Leslie Curtis and, on the corner, T & G Wills, confectioners.

The Three Pigeons public house, Portsmouth Road, in February 1954. It was demolished in the 1980s. The Courage pub was on the corner of Prospect Road. Next door was Eagle Components, plastic fabricators.

In the early 1960s the now-vanished sweet shop on the corner of Portsmouth Road and Winters Road was run by T & G Wills.

Thomas Hardy

A MONTH before Far From The Madding Crowd was published in book form, its author, Thomas Hardy, and his first wife, Emma, just back from their honeymoon, moved to St David's Villa, Hook Road, close to The Maypole, Ditton Road.

He lived there from October 1874 to March 1875.

In the icy December of 1874, Hardy visited Long Ditton Church on the 19th. He wrote: "Visited Long Ditton. Snow on the graves. A superfluous piece of cynicism in nature".

His landlord was David William Hughes — a relative, perhaps, of Rev James Roydon Hughes, the church's rector?

IN 1909, Miss May Bischoff, of Summerfield House, Ditton Hill, married the 60-year-old rector, Rev Alfred Martell. May later recalled Lewis Carroll visiting her family at Summerfield when she was about 10 years old.

She wrote in retirement: "He was a cousin of my step-mother's and as far as I can remember, he was very dull and shy. He was, of course, very fond of pretty little girls, but my sisters and I were certainly not pretty enough, or young enough, to suit his tastes!" May lived to 101.

Swinging sixties — Melodie hair stylists, G W Abel's, Clark's greengrocer's and Greenaway's.

Louis Thorn's gents' hairdresser's at 41 Fleece Road in the early 1960s and the Corner Shop.

Clark's, the greengrocer's

Elsie and Bob Clark. Elsie worked at the shop in Fleece Road for a remarkable 54 years.

BOB and Elsie Clark ran the greengrocer's in Fleece Road from 1948 until they retired to Molesey in 1985. Elsie had worked at the shop under previous owners, Ted and Mabel Andrews, since she was just 15 years of age in 1931.

Also in the parade in the 1960s was A H Greenaway's, toys and cycle shop. Here, in 1967, Ditton Hill Road resident Paul Adams, then 13, bought his treasured copy of the Beatles' Magical Mystery Tour EP. Mr Greenaway's son, Malcolm, repaired the bikes. At St Mary's Church, Malcolm's father always announced the next hymn after the rector, Rev Burt, climbed down from the pulpit.

At the Corner Shop at the Ditton Hill Road junction, Frank Gilham "always wore a dust coat and a cap and never asked what you wanted; he just raised an eyebrow." Inside his shop, there was a distinctive smell of steam from the clothes washing Mrs Gilham was busily engaged in.

Louis 'Prickly' Thorn ran the hairdresser's next to the Corner Shop. He was a prominent member of the British Legion which had its headquarters in Windmill Lane before its modern centre was opened in Betts Way. The Thorns traded in Long Ditton for many decades. Long queues built up on Saturday mornings in the 1950s and boys had to pass the time reading outdated copies of the Beano. Boys were stopped from having cuts on Saturdays when L G Wright took over in the 1960s. The business traded as Elgees in the 1970s.

Wigham's fishmonger's and Scott's confectioner's in the 1960s.

Thistle cleaners, and next door, the Handy Shop run by Mrs Hillard.

Bertram Wigham's fishmonger's, Scott's confectioner's, and the smell of stew...

DURING the summers of the 1950s and 1960s, children returning from school used to enjoy cooling down on hot afternoons with penny orange lollies purchased at Scott's confectioner's at 49 Fleece Road. It seemed to be the only place that stocked such a treat.

The boys and girls would be served by a tall, friendly and bespectacled shopkeeper, Mr Stanley Albert Boyles. Mr Boyles ran the shop for many of the post-war years before retiring in about 1970. He was helped in the store by his wife.

Another of Mr Boyles' successful lines was Quality Street chocolates. For many years, these sweets were kept in a revolving trans-

parent drum. One regular customer with a liking for Quality Street was Harry Adams, who lived at 80 Ditton Hill Road. When Mr Boyles saw him approaching the shop on a bicycle, he would weigh out the chocolates in advance. But Harry wasn't too keen on being seen as predictable. And on one occasion Harry deliberately asked for something different to fool Mr Boyles.

One former villager affectionately recalled Mr Boyles as a "very pleasant, affable bloke".

Locals remember a Mr Scott running the sweet shop in earlier times. In the 1990s, the premises traded as the Pacific Building Supplies.

Bertram Wigham's fish and chip shop at 47 Fleece Road was very popular. It also sold a good selection of wet fish. Rock salmon and fish cakes to fry at home were fast lines. On the wall in a glass case was a stuffed fish caught at Boxmoor in Hertfordshire. In the 1960s, customers would ask for "six'a'chips" — a portion of chips costing 6d, wrapped in newspaper. Piles of coley were also for sale, bought for pets.

The Handy Shop, run by silver-haired Mrs B M Hillard at this time, traded as a draper. She sold haberdashery items such as cottons, wools, needles and thread. An abiding memory of villagers was the seemingly daily smell of stew and onions in the shop.

A 152 bus destined for Hampton Court approaches the Woodstock Lane junction of the Kingston bypass in about 1961.

Opening of the Hook underpass on the Kingston bypass

LONG Ditton's countryside around Woodstock Lane was split in two when the Kingston bypass was built in the late 1920s.

Work on the bypass construction by Surrey County Council commenced in 1924. Problems with horse-drawn transport had been causing chaos on roads around the London area and this led to plans to build the road. It was hoped that motor vehicles, being swifter than horse-drawn ones, would solve the problem of congestion, but this optimism was short-lived. On the Portsmouth Road near Long Ditton, there had been a 25 per cent increase in traffic between 1913 and 1925.

Over the years, the use of the motor cars increased dramatically and by the early 1950s, long queues of traffic built up in the rush hours between Woodstock Lane North and the Hook roundabout.

In order to ease the frustrating jams at the roundabout, an underpass was constructed in the late 1950s. It was opened on 12th February 1960 and was the first of its type in Britain. A model of the underpass is displayed at the Science Museum in London. In the first year of use, the road surface in the underpass was heated to prevent the surface freezing but this costly scheme was soon abandoned.

One of the first road accidents on the new bypass was in December 1928 and it involved Lord Beaverbrook. His chauffeur-driven car was involved in a collision with a van at the Hook Road junction. Lord Beaverbrook, his chauffeur and private secretary were all injured.

Doris Palmer, a cashier at the Ace of Spades garage, later received a £25 cheque from the VIP for attending to the casualties. Miss Palmer had bathed Lord Beaverbrook's hand and applied iodine to the wound.

And in a letter to the Prime Minister, Stanley Baldwin, Lord Beaverbrook said he was so grateful to be alive, he was handing out £25,000 to good causes. Surbiton Hospital received £1,000.

From the Kingston bypass, Long Ditton was served with another range of buses from far and wide.

Passengers could board a 72 bus to Esher (the Windsor Arms) or in the other direction to Tolworth and East Acton, while the 152 ran from Feltham and Hampton Court to Mitcham.

From 1946 to 1977, the 715 Green Line also called. This ran between Guildford and Hertford and provided a useful service between Long Ditton and the West End with stops in Victoria, Oxford Circus and Regents Park.

Lovers bench

LOVERS over the years have carved their initials on the sturdy old bench under the oak tree at the junction of Woodstock Lane North and the Kingston bypass. In the above picture two ramblers take a relaxing break from dog-walking to rest on this well-worn landmark. The background shows the fields of cows near One Tree Hill before the rose nursery was established.

Manor Lodge, Woodstock Lane, c1890.

George Barnes' shop in the mid 1960s with Burgess's newsagent's next door.

Burgess newsagent's

THE Burgess family had been bringing the news to Long Ditton for nearly 40 years as the millennium approached. The family took over the Fleece Road shop in 1961 after running a newsagent's in Hook Road, Hook, for six years. Prior to this, the family had been in the newspaper retail business at Bournemouth and earlier near Bury, Lancs.

On arriving in Long Ditton, Clifford and Joan Burgess lived in Herne Road before moving to Effingham Road with son, Rae, (born 1952) and daughters Andrea and Karen. The sisters are older than Rae. Karen is the oldest.

Rae Burgess in 1979.

Since his early childhood in Hook Road, Rae had been attending Hinchley Wood Infants School. When the family moved to Effingham Road he was taught at Long Ditton School.

He returned to Hinchley Wood on reaching secondary school age.

Clifford Burgess died suddenly in 1980 and Joan passed away in 1991. In true family tradition, Rae took over the business. He had already been working in the shop since leaving school so was familiar with the trade.

For decades the store was the hub of village life around Ditton Hill. By the late 1990s, the friendly face of quietly-spoken Rae had become known to hundreds of villagers, be they early morning risers or those hurrying to buy a last minute lottery ticket.

Shoe repairer who sang while he worked

WELSHMAN George Barnes was a shoe and boot repairer in Fleece Road parade for more than 30 years.

He arrived in 1948 and by hard work and determination succeeded in keeping his business going throughout the years, supported by his many loyal customers. He once told the *Esher News and Mail* that his customers were "very, very nice, marvellous people".

One villager recalled: "He used to sing joyfully while he repaired the shoes." The repairs were carried out at the back of the shop.

George and his wife, Joan, retired to Bookham and more recently, the premises traded as Kimber's printing services. The original arch separating the back of the old shop from the front counter in the cobbler days remained, however.

In the above 1960s picture, Rectory Lane can be seen emerging into Fleece Road in its original position, just feet from the shop on the corner. In the 1970s, the road was re-routed a few yards to make a safer, staggered junction. The old part of Fleece Road now serves as a small car park for the shop customers at the back of their stores.

In 1959, about six years before this photograph was taken, George Barnes' neighbours were the newsagents, Joshua Forster, and on the corner, G Goddard, the grocer. The long-since-vanished allotments which covered a large area of the lower part of Rectory Lane can be seen behind the sign.

George Barnes.

Victims of sinking
Titanic

Austin Partner's grave at St Mary's Church.

PLAGUED by a sense of foreboding, Austin Partner, of Ewell Road, Tolworth, went aboard the ill-fated Titanic in April 1912, never to see

Austin Partner.

his friends and family in the Surbiton area again.

Mr Partner, an expert on Canadian investments, had made 16 previous transatlantic trips but this journey seemed to fill him with dread.

He embarked but with 1,513 others, drowned when the White Star liner hit an iceberg and sank on 14-15th April.

His was one of the few bodies recovered from the Atlantic. It was embalmed and sent from New York to Tilbury, Essex. On May 21 it was taken by train to St Pancras from Tilbury and on to Kingston by a car-riage and pair of horses for burial at St Mary's, Long Ditton. Originally, Tolworth was a detached part of Long Ditton parish.

Mr Partner was 40 years old at the time and left a wife, Nellie, and two young sons.

One of the stewards on the liner was Athol Broome, from Long Ditton. Less is known of him than Austin Partner. It is believed he had been married only a year when he perished in the tragedy.

His jacket, embroidered with his surname, is an important exhibit in Titanic exhibitions.

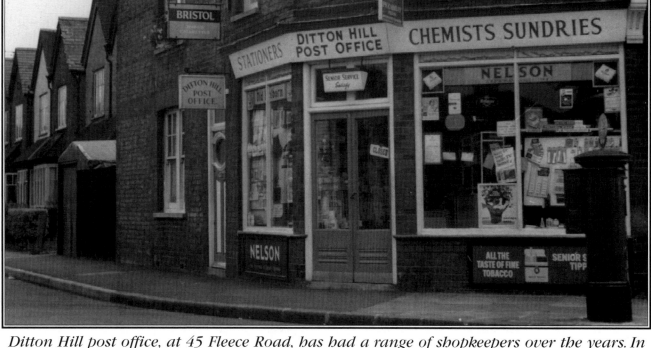

Ditton Hill post office, at 45 Fleece Road, has had a range of shopkeepers over the years. In 1965, it also sold chemist sundries as well as stationery.

Effingham Road man escapes
Survived Lusitania

EJ TOWNLEY of Holmleigh, 13, Effingham Road, Long Ditton, survived the sinking of the liner, Lusitania, off the Irish coast after a German torpedo attack in May 1915. He was rescued, but 1,200 lost their lives. When the ship was torpedoed, Mr Townley, on a business trip to America, was sitting with other passengers in the saloon, lunch having just been served. "There was a jar, the ship started to list and the glasses started tumbling off the tables,", he told the *Surrey Comet*.

"One of the most terrible sights of the whole catastrophe occurred whilst the boats were being launched. About 70 women and children got into one boat but the attempt to launch it failed. The boat hung on end by the davits and all the women and children in it dropped into the sea and were washed away."

The ill-fated liner Lusitania.

Ladies started bakery
Post Office

FLEECE Road's shopping parade appears to have been built about 1906 on land downhill from The Elms.

In June that year, George, Frederick, Harold and Thomas Barnes of the Barnes Trading Co Chiswick, sold at least part of the parade to John Brooks of London and Henry Wooff of Fulham, a wine and spirit merchant.

Indications are that the post office opened at 45 Fleece Road, on the corner of Ditton Hill Road in 1932, when business was transferred from the little shop on Ditton Hill.

In January 1956, James and Marcia Gaisford sold the business for £250 to Alfred Anderson Verity.

During the late 1950s, John Woolley and Co lived and worked at the site.

In 1962, Lily Morley, a widow, and Lena Morley, a spinster, were running the shop as a confectioner's, stationer's, and tobacconist's.

By late 1965, Mrs Florence Hull, and Ivy Rundle, a widow, both from Par Beach, Cornwall, owned the business and started selling cakes and bread.

A few years later, a Mr Sheffield took over but later moved to Malden Rushett. In 1985, Charan and Gurjit Kang for six years sold bread and children's clothes. In 1991 the shop was taken over by Mr W'Dher. The bakery section ceased.

1977

Pictures of St Mary's Junior School, Long Ditton, taken in May 1977 to mark the Queen's silver jubilee. The head was Mr P Twinn.

Some familiar faces in Long Ditton

Dutchman Ren Hendriksen ran Hill Park Nurseries from 1966 for more than 30 years.

Newsagent Rae Burgess in 1998. His family took over the shop in Fleece Road in 1961.

Toastmaster Mike Solomons, 75 Effingham Road, headed Thames TV's cameramen.

Cyril and Ethel Rook spent half their lives at Pound Close.

Fred Rainbow, born 1921 — a life-long resident of Rectory Lane.

Pat Rainbow, wife of Fred, lived in Ewell Road then Rectory Lane.

Oliver Cromwell personally handed run-down Long Ditton church £100.

Kim and Gerry Stone ran the Plough and Harrow in the 1990s as a community public house.

Richard Attenborough's family home was Four Elms, St Mary's Road, in the 1950s.

Brownies have been an important social group in Long Ditton for many years. This photograph shows some past members.

Percy Perrin, a turncock, lived in Kings Road for some 65 years before retiring to Littlehampton with his wife, Beryl. A devoted Baptist, he worked for the water board and was often seen on his bicycle.

Brian and Eva Arnold came to Fleece Road as greengrocers in May 1985. From 1970-1985, Brian ran a florist's and greengrocer's at Thames Ditton High Street. His parents, Rose and Harry, together with his brothers, Barry and Roger, ran the newsagents at Thorkhill Road from July 1966 to 1981. "It's great here. I've never regretted coming to Long Ditton." said Brian in 1998.

Class of 1998: pupils and some staff at St Mary's Junior School, Sugden Road, Long Ditton, in July 1998 with head Mrs Sue Woods (inset).

The New Inn at The Rushett, Long Ditton, soon after the coming of the steam railway in 1838.

Long Ditton's oldest standing building is The Cottage, Ditton Hill, formerly The Post Office, the Farm House, Old Farmhouse and then Cumbrae Cottage. The house, Cumbrae, next door, was pulled down in about 1962 after being turned into flats.

The Cottage, earlier known as The Dell, was demolished in 1963. Church Meadow estate replaces it.

Some Ditton gents of the past who were members of the Ditton Hill Bowling Club whose matches were played on the cricket field later acquired for the large cemetery at the top of Rectory Lane. In the bottom row, the first four men, left to right, are Mr Elliot, of the water works, (standing); Mr Steven Stokes, the builder, of Kings Road; Mr Gibson and church verger H J White. Included in the top row are Albert Pettel (second from left); Mr Baker, Mr Amos and Mr Moss from the police, plus Mr Watson.

Ferry Road showing Hammerton's and Buttery's boatyards in their hey-day.

About the author

MARK Davison spent his first 20 years living in Hook. The nearby lanes of Long Ditton were frequented by him when he reported the Elmbridge area for the Kingston Borough News after leaving school in the late 1970s.

The history of the locality also intrigued journalist Mark and features on the district by Margaret Bellars in his newspaper fuelled his fascination. He has already co-written 13 books, most with weatherman Ian Currie. They include Surrey in the Sixties and the Surrey Weather Book. His last book, Hook Remembered, he researched and wrote by himself.

Other books by the same author

HOOK REMEMBERED

Mark Davison

Hook Remembered. Published by Frosted Earth £9.95 (ISBN 0-9516710-9-x)
Surrey Weather Book. Published by Frosted Earth. £9.95 (ISBN 0-9516710-6-5)
Surrey in the Sixties. Published by Frosted Earth. £9.95 (ISBN 0-9516710-4-9)
Surrey in the Seventies. Published by Frosted Earth £9.95 (ISBN 0-9516710-7-3)
Surrey in the Hurricane. Published by Froglets £8.50 (ISBN 0-9513019-2-6)
London's Hurricane. Published by Froglets £8.50 (ISBN 0-9513019-8-5)
East Surrey Then and Now Published by Argus Books £5.95 (ISBN 1-85486-036-4)
Sussex Weather Book. Published by Froglets/Frosted Earth £10.99 (ISBN 1-872337-13-9)
Berkshire Weather Book. Published by Froglets/Frosted Earth £9.95 (ISBN 1-872337-48-1)
Hampshire Weather Book Published by Froglets/Frosted Earth £9.95 (ISBN 1-872337-20-1)
Norfolk & Suffolk Weather Published by Froglets/Frosted Earth £9.95 (ISBN 1-872337-99-6)
Kent Weather Book Published by Froglets £10.99. (ISBN 1-872337-85-6)
Red Sky At Night, Weather Sayings Published by Frosted Earth £4.95 (ISBN 0-9516710-2-2)

Telephone 01737 221215 for details on these publications